IT WAS OCTOBER 6TH HARRIS WAS ON HER WAY TO THE HOSPITAL SHE HAD A 9 POUND 15 OUNCE BABY GIRL WHO WAS BORN AT 3:59 pm WHO SHE NAMED KENEKA DENISE HARRIS.

THEN A YEAR LATTER AFTER SHELLY HAD KENEKA, KENEKA'S DAD LOST HIS LIFE DUDE TO BEING SHOT SO SHE WAS LEFT TO RAISE HER BABY GIRL ON HER OWN AS A SINGLE MOTHER ...

11 YEARS LATER KENEKA  WAS DEALING WITH LOTS OF PAIN AND HURT SHE WAS AT A POINT IN HER LIFE WHERE SHE

WISHED HER DAD WAS AROUND SADLY
HER MOMS BOYFRIEND STARED
TOUCHING ON HER AND ONE DAY HER
FATHER SHOWED UP AS A GHOST AND HE
WAS TELLING HER TO COME HERE HE
WAS TRYING TO SAVE HER BUT SHE
DIDN'T KNOW IT WAS HER FATHER AT
THE TIME SO SHE STARTED SCREAMING
AND HER MOM CAME IN THE ROOM AND
AS SOON AS HER MOM OPENED THE
DOOR THE GHOST THAT WAS HER DAD
DIAPERED AND HER MOM SAID WHATS
WRONG THEN KENEKA SAID THERE WAS
A MAN STANDING RIGHT THERE AND HER
MOM REPLIED WHERE I DON'T SEE
ANYTHING THEN HER MOTHER LEFT THE

ROOM AND KENEKA WENT BACK TO SLEEP ABOUT A HOUR LATER HER MOMS BOYFRIEND CAME IN THE ROOM AFTER HER MOM WAS SLEEP AND BEGIN DOING THINGS TO KENEKA WHILE HER MOM WAS IN THE OTHER ROOM SLEEP THE NEXT MORNING KENEKA TELLS HER MOM WHAT HAPPENED SHE SAID MOM HE PUT HIS D.I.C.K. IN MY FACE KENEKA WAS TO SCARED TO SAY THE WORD SO SHE SPELLED IT OUT AND HER MOM YELLS WHAT !!! AND GOES IN THE LIVING ROOM AND SAYS TO ANTHONEY ARE YOU TOUCHING MY DAUGHTER AND HE SAID NO THEN HER MOM REPLIES HOW DOES SHE KNOW WHAT DICK IS THEN AND SHE

SLAPS ANTHONY ACROSS THE FACE AND TELLS HIM TO GET OUT HER HOUSE NOW AND SHE STARTS CRYING ANTHONY WALKS OUT THE DOOR ... KENEKA THOUGHT SHE WAS SAFE AFTER LETTING HER MOM KNOW BUT ABOUT A WEEK LATER SHE DROPS KENEKA OFF AT ANTHONY MOMS HOUSE SO HE CAN WATCH HER SO HER MOM COULD GO TO WORK KENEKA GETS SCARED AND ABOUT A HOUR AFTER HER MOM LEFT HER WITH HIM HE TAKES HER DOWN STAIRS TO HIS ROOM IN THE BASEMENT AND BEGINS TO TOUCH HER AGAIN THIS WENT ON FOR ABOUT 6 MONTHS- A YEAR STRAIGHT KENEKA BEGAN TO GET VERY

DEPRESSED AND STARTED TO THINK HER MOM DIDN'T LOVE HER AND SHE FELT LIKE SHE WAS NOTHING AND SHE BEGAN TO THINK WHY DOESN'T MOM BELIEVE ME .... KENEKA WAS SO HURT ....  AND ANTHONY SAID TO KENEKA AFTER HE WAS DONE YOU BETTER NOT SAY NOTHING TO YOUR MOM ABOUT THIS AGAIN OR I WILL HURT YOU SO KENEKA STAYED QUIET ABOUT IT FOR ABOUT A YEAR THEN ONE DAY KENEKA'S 6TH GRADE TEACHER ASK KENEKA WHATS BEEN GOING ON .... HER TEACHER SAID YOU HAVNT BEEN YOUR SELF LATELY SO THEN KENEKA FINALLY GOT THE COURAGE TO SAY SOMETHING SHE

BROKE DOWN IN CLASS AND TOLD MS.PUTNAM SHE BEGAN TO TALK SHE SAID MY MOMS BOYFRIEND HAD BEEN TOUCHING ME AND HE SAID HE WOULD HURT ME IF I SAID ANYTHING THEN SHE BROKE DOWN CRYING PUTNAM RAPPED HER ARMS AROUND KENEKA AND SAID OMG….. YOUR GOING TO BE OK THEN MS.PUTNAM TOOK KENEKA DOWN TO THE PRINCIPALS OFFICE AND EXPLAINED TO THE PRINCIPAL WHAT WAS GOING ON BECAUSE KENEKA WAS TO SHOOK UP TO TALK ABOUT IT THEN THE PRINCIPAL SAID TO KENEKA YOU ARE GOING TO BE OK AND CALLED THE POLICE THE POLICE TOOK KENEKA TO GET CHECKED

OUT AT THE HOSPITAL THEN THEY
PLACED KENEKA IN A FOSTER HOME
KENEKA WAS SO DEPRESSED AND FELT
UN LOVED AND NEGELTED SHE WAS
REALLY WISHING HER FATHER WAS
AROUND CAUSE SHE KNEW IF HER DAD
WAS AROUND HE WOULD OF PROTECTED
HER AFTER MEETING HER FOSTER
FAMILY KENEKA LAYED IN HER BED AND
CRIED HER SELF TO SLEEP SHE FELT
LIKE SHE WAS NOTHING SHE CRIED
EVERYDAY THAT SHE WAS IN FOSTER
CARE AND TO MAKE THINGS EVEN
WORSE SHE WAS PLACED WITH PEOPLE
WHO DIDN'T EVEN CARE THAT SHE WAS
HURTING THEY WOULD TELL HER TO

STOP CRYING, CRYING AINT GOING TO DO NOTHING FOR YOU HER FOSTER MOM WAS VERY MEAN TO HER THIS WENT ON FOR ABOUT 6 MONTHS .... KENEKA WAS RETURNED TO HER MOTHER AFTER ABOUT 6 MONTHS AND ANTHONY HAD BEEN ARRESTED AND THE COPS ASKED KENEKA HOW LONG DO YOU WANNA SEE HIM IN JAIL KENEKA TOLD THEM TILL SHE WAS 18 YEARS OLD AT THE TIME KENEKA WAS 11 SO THE COPS DID WHAT KENEKA WANTED AND THEY GAVE HIM 7 YEARS IN JAIL ONCE KENEKA GOT RETURNED TO HER MOM SHELLY HER MOM TOLD KENEKA THAT SHE WAS NOT TALKING TO HIM ANYMORE AND SHE

WOULDN'T HAVE TO WORRY ABOUT HIM
ANYMORE SHE WAS DONE WITH HIM ...

ABOUT A YEAR PASSES KENEKA WOULD
ALLAYS GET THE MAIL WHILE HER MOM
WAS AT WORK AND ONE DAY KENEKA
GETS THE MAIL AND SEES A LETTER FOR
ANTHONY AND ITS FROM THE JAIL
KENEKA COULD NOT BELIEVE IT HER
MOM WAS LIEING TO HER THE WHOLE
TIME SHE WAS STILL TALKING TO THIS
MAN EVEN AFTER WHAT HE DID TO HER
DAUGHTER KENEKA BEGAN TO CRY SHE
FELT SO HURT SO KENEKA DIDN'T SAY
NOTHING TO HER MOM ABOUT IT SHE
JUST STAYED QUIET A COUPLE MONTHS

LATTER KENEKA WAS IN HER MOMS ROOM SHE WAS GOING IN HER DRESSER DRAWER TO GET SOME MONEY OUT HER MOMS COIN PURSE SO SHE COULD GO TO THE CORNER STORE TO GET SOME SNACKS AND SHE SEES A BUNCH OF LETTERS SO KENEKA DECIDES TO PICK THEM UP AND STARTS READING THEM KENEKA DECOVERED THAT HER MOM WAS ALSO GOING TO VISIT HIM IN JAIL THERE WAS A PICTURE OF HER MOM AND ANTHONY TOGETHER IN SIDE THE JAIL HE WAS AT KENEKA CRIED OUT WHAT !!!!!!! SHE COULD NOT BELIEVE HER MOM WAS REALLY STILL TALKING TO THIS MAN AND GOING TO SEE HIM IN JAIL

KENNAN PUT THE LETTERS BACK HOW
SHE FOUND THEM AND BEGAN TO CRY
SHE FELT LIKE HER MOM DINT LOVE HER
AT ALL AND KENEKA STILL STAYED
QUIET ...

A COUPLE YEARS PAST AND KENEKA WAS
STILL SEEING THE LETTERS FROM
ANTHONY COMING IN THE MAIL SHE WAS
REALLY STARTING TO GET PISSED OFF
SO WHILE KENEKA'S MOM WAS AT WORK
KENEKA PACKED HER BAG AND RAN
AWAY KENEKA RAN OFF TO HER
BOYFIRED JOHNS FRIENDS HOUSE SHE
STAYED THERE FOR AT LEAST 2 WEEKS
SHE STARTED DRINKING AND SMOKING
CIGS KENEKA'S MOM WAS VERY SCARED

SHE HAD FLYERS ALL OVER SAINT PAUL MN OF KENEKA   AND HAD A AMBER ALERT OUT FOR KENEKA AFTER 2 WEEKS OF BEING HIDDEN AT HER BOYFRIENDS ,FRIENDS HOUSE JOHNS MOM HAD LEARNED THAT KENEKA WAS AT HIS FRIENDS HOUSE SO SHE REPORTED IT TO THE POLICE AND THE POLICE SHOWED UP AT THE DOOR AND SAID WE ARE LOOKING FOR KENEKA HARRIS WE WHERE TOLD SHE WAS HERE KENEKA'S BOYFRIEND ANTHONY MOVES OUT THE POLICES WAY AND LETS THEM IN THE COP LOOKS AT KENEKA AND HER EYES GET BUCK THE COP SAYS ARE YOU KENEKA HARRIS AND KENEKA REPLIED

YES... I AM THE COPS SAID WE NEED YOU TO COME WITH US SO GET ALL YOUR STUFF TOGETHER  SO KENEKA FOLLOWS HIS INSTRUCTION AND DOES WHAT THE COP ASKED HER TO DO KENEKA THEN WALKS WITH THE POLICE  OUT TO THE COP CAR AS THE COPS DRIVE KENEKA BACK TO HER MOMS HOUSE THE COP ASK HER WHY DID YOU RUN AWAY FROM HOME AND SAYS YOUR MOM IS VERY CONCERNED ABOUT YOU KENEKA STARTS CRYING AND SAYS TO THE COP MY MOM DOESN'T LOVE ME .... THE COP REPLIES I THINK SHE DOES SHES GOT MISSING POSTER EVERY WHERE LOOKING FOR YOU AND SHE CALLED US

TO PUT OUT A AMBER ALERT ... KENEKA
JUST CRYS AND SAYS NOTHING KENEKA
SAID TO HER SELF IF SHE LOVES ME WHY
IS SHE PUTTING A MAN THAT TOUCHED
ME BEFORE ME AND WHY IS SHE STILL
TALKING TO HIM BUT SHE DIDN'T WANT
THE COP TO KNOW WHAT WAS GOING ON
BECAUSE SHE DIDN'T WANT TO HAVE TO
GO BACK TO FOSTER CARE EVER AGAIN
SO SHE STAYED QUITE ... AS THE COP
PULLS UP TO THE DOOR KENEKA MOM IS
STANDING AT THE DOOR WAITING FOR
HER TO ARRIVE ONCE KENEKA GETS
BACK UP STAIRS HER MOM BEGINS TO
YELL AT HER ASKING HER WHY SHE RAN
AWAY AND KENEKA EXPLODES KENEKA

REPLIES CAUSE YOU LIED TO ME YOU BITCH ...... KENEKA'S MOMS SLAPS HER AND SAYS I KNOW YOU DIDN'T JUST CALL BE A BITCH SHE GOES TO GRAB THE BELT AND STARTS WHOOPING KENEKA , KENEKA DOESN'T EVEN SHED ONE TEAR AND HER MOM REPLIES YOU AINT CRYING HUH AND HITS KENEKA HARDER BUT KENEKA STILL DOES NOT SHED ONE TEAR KENEKA WASN'T FEELING NO PAIN SHE WAS THAT PISSED SO HER MOM GETS TIRED AND LEAVES THE ROOM AND SHUTS THE DOOR KENEKA STAYED IN HER ROOM THE REST OF THE NIGHT CULLDING HER PLOW IN HER BED

WISHING HER DAD WAS AROUND TO
SAVE HER ...

A COUPLE YEARS PASS KENEKA IS NOW
15 YEARS OLD KENENKA BEGINS TO GET
OUT OF CONTROL AND STARTS DRESSING
WAY TO SEXY IN HOOCHIE MAMA
CLOTHES AND SEEKING ATTENTION
FROM MEN KENEKA WAS ATTRACTED TO
OLDER MEN AND SHE BEGAN TO LOOK
FOR LOVE IN MEN SO KENEKA ENDS UP
WITH LA HE WAS 29 AT THE TIME HAD
HIS OWN PLACE AND WORKED FULL
TIME KENEKA BEGINS TO STAY AWAY
FROM HOME AGAIN AT HER BOYFRIENDS
HOUSE AND STARTED SPENDING NIGHT

AWAY FROM HOME KENEKA BECAME VERY INDEPENDENT VERY FAST SHE GOT A JOB AT VALLEY FAIR THEN SHE LEFT THERE AND GOT A JOB AT BURGER KING ONCE KENEKA GOT THE JOB AT BURGER KING SHE ENDED UP GOING BACK TO HER MOMS AND GRABBED A BAG FULL OF CLOTHES AND RAN AWAY AGAIN SHE MOVED IN WITH HER NEW BOYFRIEND LA BUT WHEN LA GOT HOME FROM WORK HE SAID TO HER HMMMM WHATS ALL THIS KENEKA SAID ITS MY CLOTHES I AM STAYING HERE WITH YOU LA REPLIED I DON'T KNOW ABOUT THIS ... BUT LET KENEKA STAY ANYWAY KENEKA STARTED TO FEEL LOVE ONCE

SHE FOUND LA SHE FOUNDLY FOUND THE LOVE SHE WAS LOOKING FOR FROM HER MOM ... A COUPLE DAYS LATTER KENEKA WAS REPORTED AS A RUN AWAY AGAIN KENEKA WORKED THE 2ND SHIFT AT BURGER KING AND SHE GOT OFF AT 10PM HER MOTHER SHOWED UP AT BURGER KING ONCE KENEKA SHIFT WAS OVER AND HER MOM SAID YOUR COMING WITH ME NOW  KENEKA SAID TO HER MOM I GOTTA CLOCK OUT SO KENEKA WENT TO THE BACK AND CLOCKED OUT THEN KENEKA GRABBED HER STUFF AND RAN OUT THE BACK DOOR KENEKA GOT LUCKY A BUS WAS COMING UP THE STREET SO SHE JUMPED ON THE BUS AND

WAS ABLE TO GET AWAY FROM HER MOM AND SHE WENT BACK TO HER BOYFRIEND LA HOUSE KENEKA THOUGHT IT WAS FUNNY CAUSE HER MOM COULDN'T CATCH HER BUT AT THE CAME TIME SHE WAS REALLY HURT CAUSE HER MOM WAS STILL TALKING TO THE MAN WHO TOUCHED HER KENEKA MOM NEVER FOUND OUT WHERE SHE WAS THIS TIME ... KENEKA STAYED WITH LA HER BOYFRIEND FOR ABOUT A MONTH THEN LA TOLD KENEKA I THINK YOU NEED TO GO BACK HOME NOW SO KENEKA PACKED UP HER STUFF AND WENT BACK HOME WHEN SHE RETURNED HOME HER MOM DECIDED TO CALL HER

COUSIN JAMES TO DEAL WITH HER SO ONCE JAMES GOT ON THE PHONE HE SAID KENEKA SO YOU THINK YOU GROWN HUH ... AND THEN HE SAID SINCE YOU SO GROWN YOU CAN PACK YOUR STUFF AND GO RIGHT BACK WHERE YOU CAME FROM .... BUT LITTLE DID HER COUSIN JAMES KNOW THAT'S EXACTLY WHAT SHE WANTED TO HEAR KENEKA WAS TO HAPPY SHE WAS SCREAMING ON THE IN SIDE SHE COULD WAIT TO GET BACK TO LA"S HOUSE SHE HANDS HER MOM THE PHONE BACK AND BEGINS TO GRAB HER STUFF BUT HER MOM WAS NOT TO HAPPY WITH WHAT HE SAID TO KENEKA AT ALL SHE GETS BACK ON THE

PHONE WITH HER COUSIN JAMES AND SAYS WHY DID YOU TELL HER THAT …. KENEKA IS IN HER ROOM STILL PACKING WITH A SMILE ON HER FACE KENEKA WAS VERY INDEPENDENT AND HAD A JOB AND SO DID HER MAN LA AND HE HAD HIS OWN PLACE SO KENEKA WAS GOOD AND COULD DO WELL IN THE STREETS LIKE IT WAS NOTHING SO IT WAS NOTHING TO KENEKA … AS KENEKA HEADS OUT THE DOOR TO GO BACK TO LA'S HOUSE HER MOM LOOKS AT HER REAL HARD SHE WAS SERIOUS … BUT SHE WANTED JAMES TO HELP HER WITH THE SISTUTION SO THAT'S WHAT HE DID SO KENEKA MADE HER WAY BACK TO THE BUS STOP ONCE

KENEKA GETS BACK TO LA'S HOUSE HE ISN'T THERE HES STILL AT WORK BUT KENEKA HAD KEYS TO LET HER SELF IN SO KENEKA GOES IN AND UN PACKED HER STUFF AND STARTED CLEANING UP THE HOUSE AND GETTING DINNER STARTED FOR LA CAUSE HE WAS GETTING OFF SOON SO HE WOULD BE HOME SOON SO KENEKA PUT ON HER FAVORITE CD JOHN B. COOL RELAX AND BLASTED IT WHILE SHE WAS COOKING AND CLEANING 30 MINS LATER LA COMES HOME TO FIND THAT KENEKA CAME BACK AND HAD HER STUFF WITH HER LA LOOKS AT KENEKA WITH CONCERN AND SAYS WHAT ARE YOU DOING BACK HERE

KENEKA REPLIES MY COUSIN SAID SINCE I WAS SO GROWN I COULD GO BACK WHERE I CAME FROM SO I PACKED MY STUFF AND LEFT AND HE JUST LOOKS AT HER FOR A SECOND THEN SAYS OH OK ... THEN AS HE GETS ALL THE WAY IN THE HOUSE HE SEES THAT KENEKA HAD DINNER READY FOR HIM AND CLEANED THE HOUSE FOR HER AND HE SAYS THANKS BABE YOU DIDN'T HAVE TO DO THIS BUT KENEKA LOVED HIM AND THAT'S JUST THE WAY KENEKA WAS ... SO THEY SPENT THE REST OF THE EVENING WATCHING MOVES TOGETHER AND CUDDLING ... KENEKA WAS SO GLAD

SHE DIDN'T HAVE TO BE IN HER MOMS HOUSE ANY MORE ...

THE NEXT DAY KENEKA GOT UP AND WENT TO WORK AT HER BURGER KING JOB THAT NIGHT KENEKA'S DRAWER CAME UP SHORT BUT THEY HAD TO PEOPLE ON THAT SAME REGISTER AT THE SAME TIME AND KENEKA KNEW SHE DINT TAKE ANYTHING SO SHE TOLD HER BOSS IT WAS NOT HER THE NEXT DAY KENEKA GETS A CALL SAYING SHE WAS FIRED AND KENEKA SAID FOR WHAT I DIDN'T DO IT KENEKA WAS FURIOUS BUT THE MANGER KEPT ON SAYING SHE DID SO SHE HUNG UP ON HIM ABOUT A WEEK LATER KENEKA GOT A NOTHER JOB AT

ROSE-DALE MALL WORKING AT MS.FIELDS COOKIES ... KENEKA WAS VERY INDEPENDENT AND A GO GETTER SO SHE WASN'T GOING TO LET THE FACT THAT SHE GOT FIRED FROM BURGER KING STOP HER SHE WAS VERY MOTIVATED KENEKA ENJOYED WORKING AT MS.FIELDS COOKIES IT WAS A GREAT JOB AND SHE ALSO GO TO WORK IN THE SAME MALL AS HER BOYFRIEND LA SO THAT WAS A PLUS FOR HER THE ONLY THING SHE DID LIKE IS THAT SHE STARTED GAINING WEIGHT FROM EATING A LOT OF PEANUT BUTTER COOKIES AND ICE'S HAHAHAHAH SHE GOT WHAT EVER SHE WANTED FOR FREE

SO KENEKA WAS TEARING THEM
COOKIES UP EVERY DAY AT WORK
KENEKA WORKED AT MS.FIELDS
COOKIES FOR ABOUT 6 MONTHS THEN
SHE HEARD ABOUT ANOTHER
OPPORTUNITY THAT WAS ALSO IN
ROSEDALE MALL SO KENEKA WENT A
HEAD AND APPLIED FOR THE POSITION
TO WORK OVER NIGHT SECURITY
WATCHING THE CAMERAS OVER NIGHT
AND SURE ENOUGH KENEKA GOT THE
JOB SO NOW SHE WAS WORKING WITH
HER BOYFIRED LA OVER NIGHT HE WAS
A JANITOR AND SHE DID OVER NIGHT
SECURITY SO THEY BOTH WORKED THE
SAME HOURS AND SAME SHIFT KENEKA

WAS TO HAPPY BUT LA THOUGHT IT WAS GREAT TO UNTILL ONE NIGHT HE DECOVERED KENEKA WAS USING THE CAMERAS TO FOLLOW HIM ALL AROUND THE MALL WHILE HE WAS WORKING SHE WAS GETTING PAYED TO WATCH HER BOYFRIEND WORK KENEKA WAS TICKED LA WOULD MAKE FUNNY FACES AT THE CAMERA CAUSE HE KNEW KENEKA WAS WATCHING HIM THEY HAD A BALL WORKING AROUND EACH OTHER AT THE END OFF THERE SHIFT THEY MEANT OUT AT THE BUS STOP AND LA SAYS TO KENEKA HOW YOU GOING TO GET PAID TO SIT ON YOUR BUTT AND WATCH ME WORK ALL NIGHT KENEKA LAUGHS

VERY HARD AND SO DOES LA KENEKA REPLIES AFTER LAUGHING I GOT IT MADE HUH AND STARTS LAUGHING AGAIN VERY HARD LA SAYS YEAH OK AND STARTS LAUGHING WITH HER KENEKA WAS DOING VERY GOOD AT THIS POINT IN HER LIFE SHE GREW UP FAST BUT SHE LEARNED TO BE INDEPENDENT VERY FAST SHE STARTED LEARNING TO BE INDEPENDENT AT THE AGE OF 14 BY THE TIME SHE TURNED 18 SHE HAD IT MASTERED KENEKA KEPT JOBS ... SHE STAYED EMPLOYED WITH THE SECURITY COMPANY FOR 2 YEARS THEN THINGS GOT KINDA BAD FOR HER SHE WAS SO TIRED SHE FELL A SLEEP WHILE

WATCHING THE CAMERAS ONE NIGHT SO
SHE WAS LET GO BECAUSE OF IT ... SHE
WAS VERY MAD CAUSE SHE LOST THAT
JOB ... SHE WAS SAD FOR A WHILE BUT
SHE WIPED HER TEARS AND GOT BACK
UP TO FIGHT AGAIN IN ABOUT 2 WEEKS
KENEKA ENDED UP GETTING A JOB AT
TARGET SHE WAS A CASHIER BUT IT WAS
FOR WAY LESS AN HOUR THAN WHAT
SHE WAS MAKING AT THE SECURITY
COMPANY AT THE MALL SHE WENT
FROM 11.50 A HOUR TO 9.00 AN HOUR SHE
WAS NOT HAPPY BUT SHE KEPT MOVING
FORWARD ANYWAY ONE NIGHT AFTER
KENEKA GOT OFF OF WORK SHE GOT
BACK TO THE HOUSE BEFORE LA GOT

THERE AND SHE SEEN THE ANSWERING MACHINE BLINKING SO SHE CHECKS THE MESSAGES AND KENEKA HEARS A FEMALE ON LA'S VOICE MAIL TALKING ABOUT HOW GOOD HE WAS IN BED KENEKA WAS FURIOUS AS SOON AS LA COMES IN THE HOUSE KENEKA SAYS TO HIM SO YOU CHEATING ON ME HUH .... THEN THEY GET TO ARGUING AND LA HITS KENEKA IN THE EYE BECAUSE SHE WAS TRYING TO LEAVE HIM BECAUSE HE WAS CHEATING ON HER AFTER LA HITS HER IN THE EYE HE SAYS NOW AUNT NO BODY GONNA WANT YOU NOW WITH THAT BLACK EYE ON YOUR FACE KENEKA STARTS CRYING AND COULDN'T

BELIEVE HE WAS HURTING HER LIKE THIS AFTER 3 YEARS IN A GOOD RELATIONSHIP KENEKA JUST SITS DOWN ON THE COUCH CRYING AND SAYS WHAT DO YOU THINK MY MOM WILL DO WHEN SHE SEES THIS LA LOOKS AT HER WITH A NERVES LOOK ON HIS FACE CAUSE KENEKA WAS ONLY 17 AND LA WAS 29 SO TECHNICALLY HE WAS MESSING WITH A MINOR SO HE HAS KENEKA GET IN THE CAR AND HE DRIVES HER TO A LOCAL WALGREEN'S SO SHE CAN GET SOME FOUNDATION TO COVER UP HER EYE SO IT WOULDN'T BE SEEN THEN THEY DRIVE BACK TO THE HOUSE ONCE THEY GET BACK IN THE HOUSE LA SAYS PLEASE

DON'T TELL YOUR MOM I AM SO SORRY BABE I WONT DO IT AGAIN THEN KENEKA REPLIES OK I FORGIVE YOU ... THE NEXT DAY BEFORE LA GOT HOME FROM WORK KENEKA HAD PACKED UP HER STUFF WHILE SHE GOT A CHANCE AND GOT OUT OF HIS HOUSE AND WENT BACK TO HER MOMS KENEKA KEPT HER EYE WELL HIDDEN WITH THE MAKE UP HER MOM NEVER SEEN IT KENEKA FIGURED HER MOM DIDN'T REALLY CARE ANYWAY AFTER HOW SHE TREATED HER SO SHE JUST KEPT QUITE ABOUT IT KENEKA WAS VERY DEPRESSED FIRST HER MOM HURT HER THEN SHE GOT HURT AGAIN BY THE MAN SHE THOUGHT LOVED HER IT WAS

LIKE EVERY ONE WANTED TO HURT KENEKA THAT'S HOW SHE BEGAN TO START FEELING ABOUT PEOPLE SO AFTER SHE LEFT HIM AND WENT BACK HOME SHE WAS SINGLE FOR ABOUT 6 MONTHS KENEKA WOULD ALWAYS LEAVE HER MOMS HOUSE DOING THE DAY AND RIDE THE BUSES ALL DAY BECAUSE SHE DIDN'T WANT TO REALLY BE THERE SO SHE JUST WENT BACK HOME ONCE IT GOT DARK AND WHEN KENEKA KEPT RIDING THE BUS EVERY DAY SHE WOULD ALWAYS KEEP SEEING THIS FINE DARKSKINED BROTHER ON THE 21 ALL THE TIME HE WOULD JUST STARE AT HER EVER TIME HE SEEN HER

BUT NEVER SAID ANYTHING THEN ONE DAY KENEKA GOT ON THE BUS AND THERE HE WAS AGAIN THIS TIME KENEKA LOCKED EYES WITH HIM AND BEGAN TO STARE BACK AT HIM THIS WENT ON FOR ABOUT A COUPLE MINS KENEKA GOT OFF THE BUS AND HE KEPT GOING THE NEXT DAY KENEKA SEES HIM BEFORE SHE GETS ON THE BUS AND HE ASKED HER FOR HER NUMBER KENEKA GIVES IT TO HIM KENEKA WAS IN LOVE AT FIRST SIGHT SHE DIDN'T KNOW WHAT IT WAS ABOUT THIS BROTHER BUT SHE WAS FEELING HIM REAL HARD SO SHE ENDED UP GETTING INTO A RELATIONSHIP WITH BLACK FOR ABOUT

3 MONTHS THEN ONE DAY SHE DECIDES
SHE JUST GOING TO SHOW UP AT HIS
HOUSE CAUSE HE ONLY LIVED ABOUT 5
BLOCKS AWAY FROM HER SO IT WAS
ABOUT 8PM AT NIGHT IT WAS DARK
KENEKA STARTS WALKING DOWN TO HIS
HOUSE CAUSE SHE WANTED TO SPEND
SOME TIME WITH HER BABE BUT
KENEKA WAS IN FOR A SURPRISE WHEN
KENEKA GOT TO HIS PLACE SHE WALKED
UP TO THE WINDOW AND SHE COULD
LOOK RIGHT IN THE BASEMENT
APARTMENT WINDOW BECAUSE IT WAS
ON THE LOWER LEVEL BUT WHEN
KENEKA WALKED UP TO THE WINDOW
AND BEGAN TO LOOK IN THE WINDOW

TEARS BEGAN TO FORM IN HER EYES ...
SHE COULDN'T BELIEVE WHAT SHE WAS
SEEING SHE WAS HER MAN BLACK ON
THE FLOOR BUTT NAKED WITH ANOTHER
WOMEN KENEKA WAS DEVASTATED SHE
BEGAN TO WALK AWAY FROM THE
WINDOW CRYING SHE CRIED ALL THE
WAY HOME  THAT NIGHT ONCE AGAIN
KENEKA GOT HURT AGAIN AFTER
TRYING LOVE AGAIN SO KENEKA DID
NOT CALL BLACK ANYMORE AFTER
SEEING THAT SHE JUST LEFT HIM ALONE
AND MOVED ON   FROM CHILDHOOD ONE
UP KENEKA THOUGHT WHEN WILL THE
HURTING AND DISAPPOINTMENT STOP SO
KENEKA STAYED SINGLE FOR A WHILE

AGAIN THEN A LITTLE AFTER KENEKA TURNED 18 SHE WAS ON HER WAY TO THE AIRPORT TO HER MOMS JOB AND SHE SAT IN BACK OF THE BUS THERE WHERE 2 DUDES BACK THERE AND ONE OF THEM ASK HER TO CHECK OUT HIS MUSIC SO SHE PUT HIS CD IN HER CD PLAYER AND STARTED LISTING TO IT AFTER LISTING TO SOME OF IT SHE GAVE IT BACK AND TOLD HIM SHE LIKED IT THEN HIS BOY THAT WAS SITTING NEXT TO HIM SAID TO KENEKA DANG YOU GOT SOME SEXY EYES HIS BOY REPLIED YEAH SHE GOT THEM BEDROOM EYES THEN HE ASKED ME ARE YOU SEEING ANYONE RIGHT NOW KENEKA REPLIED NO … SO HE

ASKED FOR KENEKA NUMBER AND KENEKA GAVE IT TO HIM THE NEXT DAY SHE GETS A CALL SHE ANSWERS AND HE SAYS HEY GIRL WHATS UP KENEKA SAYS WHO IS THIS HE REPLIES THIS IS BJ THE GUY YOU MET ON THE BUS YESTERDAY SHE SAYS OH OK THEN HE SAYS SO WHATS UP AND HE BEGINS TALKING TO HER ABOUT HIM AND HIS LIFE KENEKA JUST SITS ON THE PHONE LISTENING ... AFTER ABOUT A WEEK OF TALKING TO BJ ON THE PHONE KENEKA AGREES TO MEET UP WITH HIM DOWNTOWN MPLS WHEN KENEKA GETS DOWNTOWN MPLS BJ HAS HER MEET HIM AT POPS ARCADE SO THEY HANG OUT THERE FOR A WHILE

THEN MAKE THERE WAY DOWN THE STREET TO TGI FRIDAYS THEY GET SOME THING TO EAT AND KENEKA LISTENS TO BJ TALK FOR MOST OF THE TIME THEN BJ ASKED KENEKA WHY ARE YOU SO QUITE KENEKA REPLIES THAT'S BJ JUST THE WAY I AM I OPEN UP SLOWLY BJ SAYS OOOH OK AND HE CONTUINES TO TALK ABOUT HIS LIFE AND THINGS HE IS CURRENTLY GOING THREW SO AFTER THEY HANG OUT FOR A WHILE BJ WALKS WITH KENEKA BACK TO THE BUS STOP SO SHE CAN GET BACK HOME ONCE KENEKA GETS HOME SHE THINKS ABOUT HER EVENING WITH BJ SHE REALLY DIDN'T KNOW IF BJ IS SOMEONE SHE

WANTS TO BE WITH BECAUSE HER
HEART REALLY DESIRED TO BE WITH
BLACK SHE DIDN'T WANT TO BE WITH
ANYONE ELSE OR START OVER BUT
BLACK DIDN'T FEEL THE SAME WAY
ABOUT KENEKA SO KENEKA DECIDED TO
MOVE ON AFTER ABOUT ANOTHER WEEK
KENEKA MET UP WITH BJ AT HIS SISTERS
HOUSE IN SAINT PAUL WHILE KENEKA
WAS AT HIS SISTERS HOUSE HANGING
OUT HER MOM CALLED AND ASKED HER
WHERE SHE WAS KENEKA TOLD HER SO
HER MOM CAME AND MET KENEKA UP
THE STREET FROM HIS SISTERS HOUSE
AT BURGER KING WHILE KENEKA WAS
AT BURGER KING WITH HER MOM BJ

CALLS KENEKA AND ASKED KENEKA
WHERE SHE WAS AT KENEKA TOLD BJ I
AM AT BURGER KING UP THE STREET
THEN BJ REPLIES OK I AM COMING UP
THERE KENEKA SAYS OK AND THEY
HANG UP ABOUT 5 MINUTES LATTER BJ
SHOWS UP AT BURGER KING NOT
KNOWING KENEKA WAS UP THERE WITH
HER MOM BJ COMES IN THE STORE AND
HIS EYES GET BUCK .... KENEKA SAYS
MOM THIS IS BJ AND BJ THIS IS MY MOM
KENEKAS MOM REPLIES WHAT ARE YOU
DOING WITH MY DAUGHTER YOU ARE TO
OLD FOR HER ???? AND BJ JUST LOOKS AT
KENEKA'S MOM AND SAYS HMMM I
DON'T KNOW AND HE GETS QUITE BUT

KENEKA WAS 18 AT THE TIME SO SHE WAS CONSIDERED A ADULT BUT BJ WAS 34 HE WAS 16 YEARS OLDER THAN KENEKA BUT KENEKA HAD A THING FOR OLDER MEN THAT HER MOM WAS JUST FINDING OUT ABOUT SO KENEKA AND HER MOM FINISHED  EATING THERE MEAL AND KENEKAS MOM LEFT AND ONCE KENEKA AND BJ GOT BACK TO HIS SISTERS HOUSE BJ SAYS TO KENEKA WHY YOU DIDN'T TELL ME YOUR MOM WAS WITH YOU KENEKA REPLIED I WANTED YOU TO MEET HER  HE SAID OH OK WE COULD OF WAITED A LITTLE  LONGER BEFORE I MET HER THOUGH KENEKA JUST LOOKS AT HIM  AND LAUGHS BJ

AND KENEKA GO BACK TO PLAYING
SPADES WITH HIS SISTER TASHA THEN
KENEKA HEADS HOME AROUND 8PM
THAT NIGHT AFTER GETTING TO KNOW
BJ MORE AFTER BEING FRIENDS KENEKA
DECIDES TO GO AHEAD AND BE BJ'S
GIRLFRIEND ABOUT A YEAR INTO THE
RELATIONSHIP KENEKA FINDS OUT THAT
BJ  WAS HOMELESS AND HAS BEEN FOR A
COUPLE YEARS BUT SHE DON'T THINK
NOTHING OF IT  AND STILL STICKS WITH
HIM THE SECOND YEAR IN TO THE
RELATIONSHIP KENEKA BEGINS TO TRY
AND HELP HIM OUT SO SHE ASKS HER
MOM IF BJ CAN STAY WITH HER AND HER
MOM AND SISTER KENEKAS MOM LOOKS

AT HER CRAZY AT FIRST BUT THEN SHE AGREED TO HELP BJ OUT SO FOR ABOUT A YEAR BJ IS LIVING WITH KENEKA AND HER MOM AND SISTER ABOUT A YEAR AFTER THAT KENEKAS MOM TOLD KENEKA BJ GOT TO GO SO BJ WENT BACK TO THE HOMELESS SHELTER SO KENEKA WOULD GO TO THE SHELTER EVERYDAY TO SEE HIM  THIS WENT ON FOR ABOUT ANOTHER 2 YEARS THEN IN 2003 KENEKA AND BJ FOUND A PLACE ON FRANKLIN AVE IN SOUTH MPLS SO THEY MOVED IN TOGETHER SHORTLY AFTER MOVING IN WITH BJ KENEKA REALIZED BJ HAD SOME ANGER ISSUES AND HE WAS VERY INSECURE ,CONTROLLING AND LAZY  AT

THE TIME KENEKA HAD A JOB AT THE AIRPORT AT MC DONALD'S SHE WORKED A FULL SHIFT THEN CAME HOME TO A DIRTY HOUSE AFTER CLEANING IT BEFORE SHE LEFT FOR WORK BJ WOULD SIT IN THE HOUSE ALL DAY PLAYING THE GAME AND EATING UP HER FOOD AND WASN'T CLEANING UP SO ONCE KENEKA CAME HOME FROM WORK SHE HAD TO COOK AND CLEAN LIKE SHE HAD A KID IN THE HOUSE THIS WENT ON FOR A WHILE THEN ONE DAY KENEKA CAME HOME AND WENT OFF CAUSE SHE WAS GETTING TIRED OF BJ SITTING AROUND THE HOUSE ALL DAY DO NOTHING AND NOT BRINGING ANY MONEY TO THE TABLE TO

HELP HER WITH THE BILLS SO THEY GOT INTO IT REAL BAD CAUSE BJ DIDN'T WANT TO HEAR THE TRUTH ABOUT HIS SELF SO HE BEGAN TO ARGUE WITH HER IT GOT TO A POINT WHERE THEY WHERE ARGUING EVERYDAY BECAUSE HE DIDN'T WANT TO GET OFF HIS BUTT AND DO ANYTHING AND THE FOLLOWING WEEK BJ STARED ACCUSING KENEKA OF CHEATING SAYING STUFF LIKE HOW YOU BEEN TALKING TO AT WORK AND THERE WAS ONE TIME WHEN SOME DUDE KENEKA DIDNT EVEN KNOW CAME IN THE DOOR WITH HER THAT SHE DIDN'T EVEN KNOW SOON AS SHE GOT UP TO HER APARTMENT HE SAID TO HER HOWS

THAT MAN YOU CAME IN WITH DOWN STAIRS KENEKA LOOKS AT HIM LIKE AND SAYS HELL I DON'T KNOW WHY DON'T YOU GO DOWN THERE AND ASK HIM WHO HE HIS CAUSE I DON'T KNOW HIM BUT BJ CONTINUED TO KEEP ACCUSING KENEKA OF CHEATING SAYING RANDOM STUFF THAT HE CAME UP WITH IN HIS HEAD THAT WASN'T TRUE WHEN KENEKA WASN'T NOTHING BUT FAITHFUL TO HIM EVEN THOUGH SHE DIDN'T DESERVE WHAT HE WAS PUTTING HER THREW SHE CONTINUED TO BE FAITHFUL CAUSE THAT'S WHAT SEE DOES SHE AINT THE TYPE OF GIRL TO BE OUT HERE OPENING

HER LEGS TO EVERYONE BUT BJ WAS
JUST TO
STUPID TO SEE THAT SO HE KEPT
MAKING STUFF UP IN HIS HEAD AND KEPT
ARGUING WITH HER FOR NO REASON SO
KENEKA GOT TIRED AND SHE STARED
PACKING HER STUFF SO SHE COULD
MOVE OUT BJ TOLD KENEKA SHE AINT
GOING NO WHERE AND STOPPED HER
FROM LEAVING SHE TRIED TO GET OUT
THE DOOR HE STOOD IN FRONT OF THE
APARTMENT DOOR AND WOULDN'T LET
HER OUT SO KENEKA GOT PISSED AND
TOLD HIM TO GET THE HELL OUT HER
WAY NOW BJ SAID NO I AINT KENEKA
PUT HER BAGS DOWN AND KENEKA

PUNCHED HIM SO HARD HE WENT THREW THE WOODEN DOOR THEN KENEKA JUST LOOKED AND COULDN'T BELIEVE SHE COULD HIT LIKE THAT SHE WAS NOT AWARE OF HER OWN STRENGTH BECAUSE SHE DON'T FIGHT PEOPLE SO KENEKA STOOD THERE IN SHOCK FOR A SECOND THEN SHE STARTED LAUGHING VERY HARD AND BJ SAID YOU KNOW WHAT YOU KNOW WHAT I AM CALLING THE POLICE KENEKA SAID GO AHEAD CALL THEM YOU SHOULD OF GOT OUT MY WAY INSTEAD OF TRYING TO KEEP ME HOSTAGE SO BJ CALLS THE POLICE ON HER NOT KNOWING KENEKA WAS HAPPY TO GO WITH THE POLICE THAT

WAS HER WAY TO GET OUT THE HOUSE
AND HE COULDN'T TRY TO HOLD HER
THERE THEN WITH THE POLICE PRESENT
SO KENEKA SAT DOWN ON THE CORNER
OF HER WALL AND ENJOYED HER LAST
CIGARETTE BEFORE THE POLICE GOT
THERE TO TAKE HER AWAY BJ JUST
LOOKED AT HER HE COULDN'T BELIEVE
SHE WAS REALLY SITTING THERE
WAITING FOR THE POLICE BUT SHE DID
SHE DIDN'T CARE AND IT WOULD HELP
HER HAVE SOME FREEDOM FROM
ARGUING THE REST OF THAT NIGHT
WHEN THE POLICE GOT THERE THEY
ASK ME WHATS GOING ON I TOLD THEM I
KNOCKED HIM OUT BECAUSE HE WAS

BLOCKING THE DOOR AND TRYING TO MAKE ME STAY IN THE HOUSE THEN KENEKA STOOD UP AND TURNED AROUND AND PUT HER HANDS BEHIND HER BACK AND SAID CUFF ME I AM READY LETS GO SO YOU CAN BOOK ME BJ JUST LOOKED AT KENEKA IN SHOCK KENEKA SAID TO BJ YEAH I SAID IT NOW YOU CANT STOP ME FROM LEAVING THE POLICE IS HERE NOW YOU AINT GOT A CHOICE I AM GOING OUT THE DOOR SO THEN THE POLICE TOOK KENEKA DOWN TO THERE CAR AND TOOK HER IN FOR BOOKING BJ COMES DOWN BEHIND THE POLICE AND BEGS THEM NOT TO TAKE HER IN AND SAYING PLEASE LET HER GO I DON'T

WANNA FILL CHARGES BUT THE COP SAYS TO LATE NOW WE GOTTA BOOK HER KENEKA WAS SO HAPPY TO GO TO JAIL THAT NIGHT BECAUSE SHE DIDN'T HAVE TO DEAL WITH HIS ARGUING ALL NIGHT THE NEXT DAY BJ SHOWS UP IN THE COURT ROOM AND SAYS TO THE JUDGE I DON'T WANT TO FILE CHARGES SO KENEKA GETS TO GO FREE AND THEY DROPPED THE 3RD DAGREE ASSAULT CHARGES ON KENEKA THE NEXT MORNING WHEN KENEKA AND BJ GOT BACK TO THERE APARTMENT THEY FOUND A EVICTION NOTICE ON THERE APARTMENT DOOR IT SAID DUDE TO PROPERTY DAMAGE AND FIGHTING THEY

HAD TO MOVE BJ WAS MAD AND SAID TO KENEKA SEE NOW WE GOTTA MOVE KENEKA REPLIDED SEE NOTHING IF YOU WOULDNT HAVE TRYED TO BLOCK ME FROM LEAVING WE WOULNDT HAVE TO MOVE OUT... BJ COULDNT SAY ANYTHING HE JUST LOOKED AT KENEKA THEN KENEKA BEGAN TO PACK HER STUFF UP SHE WAS GLAD THEY HAD TO MOVE SO SHE WOULDN'T HAVE TO BE AROUND BJ AND HIS MENTAL AND VERBAL ABUSE ANY MORE SO KENEKA GRABED HER THINGS AFTER GETTING EVERYTHING PACKED AND WENT BACK TO HER MOMS HOUSE AND BJ HAD TO GO BACK TO THE SHELTER KENEKA STILL HAD KEYS TO

HER MOMS HOUSE SO SHE WAS ABLE TO LET HER SELF IN WHILE HER MOM WAS STILL AT WORK WHEN KENEKAS MOM GOT HOME SHE SAID OOH YOUR BACK AND KENEKA REPLIED YEAH I GOT PUT OUT OF MY PLACE CAUSE BJ BLOCKED ME FROM GETTING OUT THE DOOR SO I PUNCHED HIM AND HE WENT THREW THE DOOR AND THE WHOLE DOOR CAME OFF KENEKAS MOM STARTED LAUGHING VERY HARD SHE WAS TICKED THEN SHE REPLIED OK THEN KENEKA WENT BACK TO HER ROOM SHE WAS FEELING VERY DEPRESSED AND THOUGHT TO HER SELF WHEN WILL THE HURT STOP HERE SHE IS AT AGE 20 AND STILL GOING THREW PAIN

FIRST HER CHILD HOOD NOW SHES DEALING WITH HURT FROM MORE MEN IN HER ADULT HOOD KENEKA JUST LAYED IN BED THE REST OFF THE EVENING WATCHING TV IN HER ROOM THE NEXT MORNING KENEKA GETS UP AND GETS DRESSED SO SHE CAN GO OUT AND FIND ANOTHER PLACE TO MOVE TO SO KENEKA GOES TO THE LIBRARY TO GET ON THE COMPUTER SHE STARTS LOOKING FOR PLACES ON CRAIGS LIST SHE DIDNT REALLY FIND NOTHING SHE COULD AFFORD BY HER SELF SO SHE TRIED TO FIGURE OUT WHERE ELSE SHE COULD LOOK FOR A PLACE BUT SHE COULDN'T THINK OF NOTHING AT THE

TIME SO KENEKA TOOK A COUPLE BUS RIDES AND THEN SHE RETURNED BACK TO HER MOMS HOUSE WHEN SHE GOT HOME SHE TURNED ON THE TV AND A COMMERCIAL SHOWED UP THAT WAS TALKING ABOUT JOB CROPS AND THEY HAD LIVE ON SITE HOUSING SO KENEKA CALLED THE NUMBER THAT WAS ON TV TO GET MORE INFORMATION AFTER TALKING TO THEM ON THE PHONE KENEKA FOUND OUT THAT SHE WAS ABLE TO JOIN THE PROGRAM SO SHE HAD A APPOINTMENT SET UP TO GO IN 2 DAYS LATER KENEKA WAS SO EXCITED AND READY TO GET BACK OUT HER MOMS HOUSE AGAIN LATER THAT

EVENING BEFORE HER MOM GOT HOME THE DOOR BELL RING SO SHE STOOD AT THE TOP OF THE STAIRS AND PEEKED DOWN TO SEE WHO IT WAS ... WHEN SHE LOOKED AND SEEN WHO IT WAS SHE SAID TO HER SELF HERE WE GO IT WAS BJ AT HER MOMS DOOR SHE WENT DOWN THE STAIRS TO OPEN THE DOOR AND BJ SAID WHATS UP I CAME BY TO SEE YOU KENEKA REALLY DIDNT WANT TO BE BOTHERED BUT SHE LET HIM COME IN ANYWAY SOON AS BJ GETS IN THE HOUSE HE STARTS WITH HER ONCE AGAIN HE STARTS ACCUSEING HER OF BEING WITH SOME DUDE BUT KENEKA AINT DID NOTHING BUT BEEN OUT TALKING CARE

OF HER BUSINESS AND TRYING TO FIND A PLACE SO KENEKA REPLISES WHATS WRONG WITH YOU I AINT NO HOE AND YOU JUST TO STUPIED TO SEE WHAT YOU GOT I BET YOU WILL RELIZED HOW GOOD I AM IF I WALK AWAY WONT YOU ... THEN BJ JUST SITS THERE AND LOOKS AT HER WITH A STUPIED LOOK ON HIS FACE AND GETS QUIET ... KENEKA SAYS YEAH THATS WHAT I THOUGHT DON'T COME TO MY MOMS HOUSE WITH THAT MESS AND KENEKA STATRS WATCHING TV AND GETS QUIET THEN KENEKA BEGANS TO THINK TO HER SELF I WISH BLACK WOULD OF REALIZED HE HAD A GOOD WOMEN CAUSE THATS WHERE I

REALLY WANNA BE I CANT STAND THIS CLOWN ... THEN KENEKA HEARS KEYS OPENING THE DOOR HER MOM WAS NOW HOME FROM WORK WHEN HER MOM GETS UP STAIRS SHE SEES BJ AND LOOKS AT HIM LIKE HES CRAZY THEN SAYS HI BJ AND BJ SAYS HI HOW WAS YOUR DAY KENEKAS MOM REPLIES IT WAS OK AND BJ SAYS THATS GOOD ABOUT 30 MINTUES LATER BJ LEAVES TO GO BACK TO THE SHELTER AND KENEKA PROCEEDED TO HER ROOM TO GO TO BED FOR THE NIGHT THE NEXT MORING HER MOM LEFT FOR WORK AND ABOUT 30 MINTURES AFTER HER MOM LEFT THE DOOR BELL RING SHE WENT TO PEEK

FROM THE TOP OFF THE STAIRS TO SEE WHO IT WAS ... SHE SAID OMG ... IT WAS BJ AGAIN SO THIS TIME KENEKA DIDNT ANSWER THE DOOR BUT BJ WOULDNT QUIT RINGING THE BELL HE STARTED BANGING ON THE DOOR HARD AND RINGING THE BELL LIKE CRAZY KENEKA STILL DIDN'T ANSWER THEN BJ WALKED TO KENEKAS WINDOW IN THE BACK AND STARTED YELLING KENEKA !!!! HE YELLED HER NAME MANY TIMES BUT KENEKA STILL DIDNT ANSWER THEN HE BEGAN TO THROW ROCKS UP AT KENEKAS WINDOW SEVERL TIMES KENEKA STILL DIDNT RESPOND KENEKA SAID TO HER SELF OMG THIS DUDE IS A

STALKER ...... THEN BJ GOES BACK TO THE FRONT AND STARTS RINGING THE BELL AGAIN KENEKA STILL DIDNT ANSWER THEN KENEKAS MOMS LANDLORD THAT STAYED DOWN STAIRS SAID TO BJ WHO YOU LOOKING FOR HE SAID TO HER KENEKA !!!! THEN SHE REPLIED WELL I DONT THINK SHES UP THERE I DONT HEAR NO MOVING AROUND OR TV ON UP THERE AND BJ SAID YEAH OK SHES THERE AND HE BEGAN TO WALK AWAY KENEKA WAS SITTING BY THE LIVING ROOM WINDOW THAT WAS OPEN LISTENING TO EVERYTHING KENEKA THEN SIGHED WITH RELIEF ... ABOUT A HOUR LATER

KENEKS GOT DRESSED AND DESIDED TO GET OUT AND ENJOY SOME AIR ONCE SHE GOT AROUND THE CONER FROM HER HOUSE THERE WAS BJ SITTING AT THE STORE SHE LOOKED WITH SHOCK ON HER FACE SHE COULDNT BELIEVE HE WAS STILL AROUND HER HOUSE WAITING TO SEE IF SHE CAME OUT SHE KEPT WALKING BJ YELLED YO.... KENEKA !!!!!! BUT KENEKA KEEPS WALKING TO THE BUS STOP SHE LOOKS BACK AND HE WAS FOLLOWING HER KENEKA SAYS YOU DONT GOT NOTHING BETTER ELSE TO DO BUT SIT AROUND MY HOUSE AND STALK ME ... BJ SAYS NO I DONT KENEKA JUST LOOKS AT HIM WITH DISGUSTS AS THE

BUS PULLS UP KENEKA GETS ON TO GO TO HER APPOINTMENT AT JOB CROP AND BJ GETS ON TO …. KENEKA SITS DOWN IN A SEAT WHERE HE CANT SIT NEXT TO HER AND SHE BLAST HER WALKMAN AND STARTS JAMMING TO HER MUSIC … THE WHOLE TIME BJ IS JUST SITTING THERE MUGGIN HER KENEKAS STOP COMES UP SHE GETS OFF TO GET ON ANOTHER BUS TO GET TO HER DETESTATION WHEN KENEKA GETS OFF THE BUS BJ GETS OFF TO KENEKA WALKS AHEAD OF HIM TO THE BUS STOP ACROSS THE STREET TO GET ON HER NEXT BUS SOON AS KENEKA APPROACH THE BUS STOP SHE PULLS OFF HER HEADPHONES AND YELLS WHY ARE

YOU FOLLOWING ME !!!! BJ REPLIES CAUSE I CAN !!!! THEN KENEKA REPLISE WELL I AM HEADED TO MY APPIONTMENT AT JOB CROP SO I DONT KNOW WHAT YOUR GOING TO DO CAUSE YOU CANT BE WITH ME FOR THAT ... BJ JUST LOOKS AT HER .. THE BUS PULLS UP AND KENEKA GETS ON BJ ALSO GOT ON WHEN KENEKAS STOP CAME UP SHE GOT UP AND GOT OFF THE BUS PULLS OFF KENEKA LOOKS BEHIND HER TO SEE THAT BJ STAYED ON THE BUS KENEKA WAS RELIVED .... KENEKA HEADS TO THE OFFICE BUILDING AND GOES TO THE DESK TO CHECK IN THEY TELL HER TO HAVE A SEAT AND SHE WAITS ABOUT 5

MINUTES THEN THEY COME OUT TO GET HER KENEKA GOES THREW ABOUT A HOUR LONG PROSSES THE CHECK HER READING LEVEL AND MATH LEVEL AND HAVE HER WATCH A ORIENTATION VIDEO AFTER THAT THEY TELL KENEKA SHE IS IN FOR THE GED PROGRAM AND THE NURSING ASSISTANT PROGAM CLASS AND KENEKA WAS ABLE TO LIVE ON SITE THEY TOLD KENEKA SHE STARTS NEXT WEEK ... KENEKA WAS FILLED WITH EXCITEMENT KENEKA SHAKES THERE HAND AND THEY SAID TO HER SEE YOU MONDAY MORNING KENEKA SAYS OK THANKS AND HEADS OUT TO THE BUS STOP AS SHES WALKING SHE BEGINS TO

LOOK AROUND WONDERING IF BJ WAS SOME WHERE AROUND WAITING FOR HER TO COME OUT BUT SHE DIDN'T SEE HIM ANY WHERE AROUND AND SHE CONTINUED WALKING TO THE BUS STOP SHE LOOKED AT THE BUS SCHDULE AND SEEN SHE HAD 10MINS BEFORE THE BUS CAME SO SHE LIT UP A CIGARETTE AND DANCED TO HER MUSIC SHE WAS TO HAPPY THAT SHE WAS MOVING NEXT WEEK ... SHE BORADED THE BUS ONCE SHE GOT THERE AND BEGIN TO HEAD BACK HOME TO HER MOMS HOUSE ABOUT 4 HOURS LATER HER MOM CAME IN THE DOOR IT WAS FRIDAY EVENING AS SOON AS HER MOM GOT IN SHE TOLD

HER MOM THE GOOD NEWS SHE SAID MOM I WILL BE MOVING OUT AGAIN I GOT EXCEPTED IN THE GED AND NURSING PROGRAM AT JOB CORP AND I GET TO LIVE ON SITE IN A ROOM I START MONDAY MORNING HER MOM REPLIED OK .... THATS GOOD KENEKA REPLIED YES IT IS ... WITH A BIG SMILE ON HER FACE SHE WAS READY TO GO .... KENEKA SAT IN THE HOUSE FOR THE REST OF THE WEEKED WATCHING MOVES IN HER ROOM NEXT THING SHE KNOWS SHE GETS A TEXT FROM BJ SAYING HES SORRY FOR EVERYTHING HE HAD DONE TO HER AND KENEKA REPLIES YEAH OK. THE NEXT AFTERNOON BJ SHOWS UP HER

MOMS HOUSE HER MOM ANSWERED THE DOOR AND LET HIM IN KENEKA WAS JUST FINNISHING UP HER LUNCH WHEN HE GOT THERE ABOUT 30 MINUTES LATER KENEKAS MOM SAYS TO KENEKA ILL BE BACK I NEED TO RUN UP TO RAINBOW FOODS KENEKA SAYS OK HER MOM THEN LEAVES OUT TO GO GET THE BUS KENEKA AND BJ SITTING THERE WATCHING TV BJS PHONE RINGS AND HE LOOKS AT IT AND GETS UP AND WALKS TO THE BACK OF THE HOUSE WHERE THE KICTHEN WAS KENEKA OVER HEARS HIM TALKING SEXUAL TO ANOTHER WOMEN AND LAUGHING WITH HER ON THE PHONE SO KENEKA CREEPS UP TO THE

KICTHEN DOOR AND JUST STANDS THERE
HIDDEN TILL HE GETS OFF THE PHONE
THEN AS BJ COMES BACK THREW THE
KICTHEN DOOR KENEKA SWINGS AT HIM
WITH A LEFT HOOK AND HE FALLS DOWN
TO THE FLOOR HOLDING HIS FACE
KENEKA BEGANS TO SPEAK.. HOW YOU
GOING TO ACUSSE ME OF CHEATING AND
YOU GOT A FEMALE CALLING YOU AND
YOU TALKING LIKE THAT TO HER ON
THE PHONE BJ JUST LOOKS UP AT HER HE
COULDNT BELIEVE SHE HIT HIM AGAIN
AND BJ SAYS NOTHING THEN KENEKA
BEGANS TO SPEAK AGAIN SHE SAYS YOU
KNOW WHAT GET OUT MY MOMS HOUSE
NOW !!!! GO TO THAT FELMAES HOUSE

YOU WAS JUST TALKING TO ON THE PHONE I AM GOOD .... AND BJ BEGANS TO GET OFF THE FLOOR AND HE GRABS HIS STUFF OFF THE COUCH AND LEAVES KENEKA GOES BACK TO THE COUCH AFTER HE LEAVES AND BEGINS TO CRY AND SAYS TO HER SELF LIFE JUST WONT STOP BRINGING ME PAIN WHY ME ...... KENEKA CALMS DOWN AFTER ABOUT A HOUR OF CRYING SHE THEN GOES OUT TO HAVE A CIGARETTE AND BEGINS THINKING ABOUT HER LIFE SHE SAYS TO HER SELF WHAT KINDA LIFE IS THIS I GET TOUCHED AS A CHILD  AS A PRE TEEN I HAD THIS MAN FLASHING HIS DICK AT ME WHILE I AM STANDING AT

BUS STOP EVERY MORNING BUT I COULDN'T TELL MY MOM ABOUT THAT CAUSE SHE DIDN'T BELIEVE ME THE FIRST TIME I TOLD HER NOW I GOT THESE MEN HURTING ME GOD WHY ME KENEKA SCREAMS !!!!!! KENEKAS MOMS LANDLORD COMES OUT SIDE AND SAYS TO KENEKA ARE YOU OK ..... KENEKA REPLIES YEAH I AM FINE .... THE LANDLORD REPLIES YOU SURE ??? KENEKA SAYS YEAH I AM OK ... SO THE LANDLORD SAID OK ...... AND WENT BACK IN THE HOUSE AND KENEKA THEN GOES BACK IN THE HOUSE AND GETS HER STUFF PACKED SO SHE CAN BE READY TO GO TO JOB CROP IN THE MORNING WHEN

THEY COME TO GET HER . THE NEXT MORNING KENEKA GETS UP AND GETS READY TO GO HER RIDE ARRIVES AT 9AM SHE GRABBED HER STUFF AND WENT DOWN TO THE VAN SHE LOADS HER STUFF AND THE DRIVER THEN HEADS BACK TO JOB CROP WHEN SHE GETS THERE SHE IS GREETED BY THE HOUISING MANGER AND THEY SHOW HER TO HER ROOM AND GIVE HER HER KEYS AND THEY TELL HER TO GET ALL HER STUFF PUT AWAY IN HER ROOM AND COME BACK TO THE OFFICE WHEN SHES DONE KENEKA REPLIES OK... THE HOUSING MANGER LEAVES OUT THE ROOM KENEKA THEN LOOKS AROUND

THE ROOM AND THEN SITS ON THE BED AND BEGINS TO SMILE SHE WAS SO HAPPY TO BE OUT HER MOMS HOUSE AND BACK ON HER OWN AGAIN  BUT KENEKA DIDN'T LIKE THAT SHE HAD TO SHARE THE ROOM WITH ANOTHER GIRL BUT IT BEAT BEING AT HER MOMS WHERE SHE DIDN'T FEEL LOVED .... AFTER PUTTING HER THINGS AWAY KENEKA HEADED BACK DOWN TO THE OFFICE AND THEY WALKED HER TO HER FIRST CLASS FOR GED MATH AND READING  SHE WAS IN GED MATH AND READING FOR ABOUT 2 HOURS THEN SHE WENT TO LUNCH AFTER LUNCH SHE WENT TO HER NURSING ASSISTANT CLASS THAT WAS

ABOUT A HOUR LONG AT THE END OF HER FIRST DAY SHE WAS KINDA LIKING IT WHEN THE DAY WAS OVER SHE WENT BACK TO HER ROOM AND WHEN SHE WENT IN HER ROOM SHE MET HER ROOMATE HER ROOMATE SAID HI MY NAME IS LISA WHATS YOUR NAME KENEKA REPLIED HI MY NAME IS KENEKA LISA RESPONED HI KENEKA ITS NICE TO MEET YOU KENEKA REPLIED BACK NICE TO MEET YOU TO   AS TIME WENT ON KENEKA GOT MORE COMFORTABLE WITH HAVING A ROOM MATE BUT KENEKA STAYED QUITE MOST OF THE TIME WHEN SHE WAS IN THE ROOM WITH HER SHE DIDNT HAVE MUCH

TO SAY AT ALL SHE WOULD LISTEN TO HER MUSIC OR DO HOMEWORK TILL IT WAS TIME FOR LIGHTS OUT AT 10PM EVERY NIGHT KENEKA WAS AT JOB CROP FOR ABOUT 8 MONTHS AND ALSO GOT TO TAKE A DRIVING CLASS WHERE SHE COULD GO ON THE ROAD AND GET SOME DRIVING LESSONS AS WELL KENEKA WAS DOING GREAT AT JOB CROP SHE STAYED TO HER SELF AND BEING SHE WAS DOING SO GOOD WHEN THE SINGLE PERSON ROOM BECAME OPEN KENEKA WAS ABLE TO MOVE TO A ROOM BY HER SELF WITH NO ROOMMATE KENEKA WAS SO HAPPY SHE FINALLY GOT HER OWN ROOM BUT THE

NEXT WEEK THINGS TOOK A TURN FOR THE WORSE KENEKA WAS IN HER ROOM GETTING DRESSED FOR BED AND THE HOUSING MANGER WAS KNOCKING ON THE DOOR TO DO CHECKS TO MAKE SURE PEOPLE WHERE IN THERE ROOM AT 10PM THE HOUSING MANGER KNOCKED ON KENEKAS DOOR AND BEFORE KENEKA COULD ANSWER THE WOMEN PUT HER KEY IN THE DOOR AND OPENED IT AND WALED IN ON KENEKA WHEN SHE WAS NOT DRESSED KENEKA GOT PISSED AND WENT DOWN TO THE HOUSING OFFICE AND REPORTED IT THEY TOLD KENEKA THEY WOULD TALK TO THE WOMEN ABOUT IT THEN THINGS

WENT BETTER FOR A COUPLE DAYS THEN
ALL OF A SUDDEN THE HOUSING MANGER
JUST WALKS IN ON KENEKA AGAIN THIS
TIME KENEKA WAS DRESSED BUT
KENEKA WAS STILL STARTING TO GET
KINDA PISSED SHE BEGAN TO FEEL LIKE
THE LADY WAS DOING IT ON PURPOSE
BUT KENEKA STAYED COOL THE NEXT
NIGHT KENEKA HAD JUST CAME OUT THE
SHOWER AND SHE WAS WALKING BACK
TO HER ROOM AND THE HOUSING
MANGER SEEN HER LEAVING THE
SHOWER SO KENEKA GOES TO HER
ROOM AROUND 945PM TO DRY OFF AND
GET HER NIGHT CLOTHES ON THIS TIME
THE LADY DIDNT KNOCK SHE JUST

TURNED THE KEY AND CAME RIGHT IN WITH OUT WARNING AND IT WASNT TIME FOR HER TO CHECK TILL 10PM SHE WAS EARLY KENEKA SNAPPED AND CALLED THE WOMEN ALL OUT HER NAME AND TOLD HER SHE WAS GOING TO BEAT HER UP  THE LADY HURRYED UP AND SHUT THE DOOR KENEKA THREW SOME CLOTHES ON AND STORMED DOWN TO THE OFFICE  AND THREATED THE LADY SOME MORE ALL OF A SUDDEN THE LADY GOT SMART BACK AT KENEKA WHEN SHE WAS AROUND HER CO WORKERS BUT SHE DIDNT HAVE NOTHUNG TO SAY WHEN SHE WAS UP AT KENEKAS ROOM BARGING IN ON KENEKA  THE STAFF

TOLD KENEKA HER BEHAVIOR WAS NOT ACCEPTABLE AND KENEKA SAID TO THE STAFF I REPORTED HER AND YALL STILL AINT DOING NOTHING ABOUT IT SO I WILL THE STAFF SAID TO KENEKA PLEASE RETURN TO YOUR YOUR AND WE WILL TALK TOMMROW WHEN THE DAY STAFF COMES IN KENEKA LOOKED AT THEM ANGRILY AND WENT BACK UP TOWARDS HER ROOM AND ONE OF THE GIRLS STOPPED KENEKA IN THE HALL WAY AND SAID CAN I TALK TO YOU FOR A MINUTE KENEKA SAID YEAH ... SURE SO SHE WENT BACK TO THE GIRLS ROOM WITH HER AND THE GIRL BEGAIN TO TELL KENEKA THAT WOMEN THAT

WALKED IN ON YOU LIKES WOMEN
KENEKA YELLED WHAT!!!!!!!! THE
REPLIED SHHHHH ! YEAH SHE KEPT
DOING IT TO ME TO WHEN I FIRST CAME
HERE BUT SHE STOPPED KENEKA SAID
OK WELL SHE GOT THE RIGHT ONE
CAUSE I AINT GOING FOR IT AND KENEKA
THANKED THE GIRL FOR LETTING HER
KNOW AND KENEKA WENT BACK TO HER
ROOM AND WENT TO BED THE NEXT
MORNING KENEKA MET WITH STAFF
FIRST THING IN THE MORNING AND THEY
TOLD HER SHE WAS PUT OUT BECAUSE
SHE THREATENED STAFF KENEKA SAID
YOU NEED TO FIRE HER SHE
DISRESPECTING PEOPLE UP IN HERE

STAFF SAID WE UNDERSTAND THAT AND WILL BE DOING A INVESTIGATION ON HER BUT YOU STILL HAVE TO LEAVE KENEKA REPLIED OK ... AND WENT TO PACK HER STUFF AND WENT DOWN TO THE MAIN OFFICE TO TURN IN HERE KEYS AND WHILE SHE WAS IN THERE SHE NOTICE THERE WAS A PICTURE OF HER ON THE WALL THAT SAID IF YOU SEE HER ON THIS PROPERTY CALL THE POLICE IMMEDIATELY KENEKA WAS SHOCKED AND THOUGHT TO HER SELF WOW... THEY THAT SCARED OF ME HUH.... AND KENEKA HANDED HER KEYS OVER TO THE LADY AND WALKED OUT THE DOOR AND WENT TO GO GET ON THE BUS BACK

TO HER MOMS HOUSE WHEN KENEKA
GOT BACK HER MOM WAS HOME SHE
TOLD HER MOM WHAT HAPPENED AND
HER MOM JUST SAID OK LIKE ALWAYS
AND KENEKA WENT BACK TO HER ROOM
AND UNPACKED HER STUFF  AFTER
GETTING EVERTHING UN PACKED
KENEKA STAYED IN HERE ROOM THE
REST OF THE DAY CRYING ONCE AGAIN
AND WONDERING WHY BAD THINGS KEEP
HAPPENING TO HER WHEN SHE IS SUCH A
GOOD PERSON SO THE NEXT MORNING
KENEKA GOT UP AND WENT BACK OUT
TO FIGHT FOR WHAT SHE NEEDED AGAIN
KENEKA HAD HER BREAKDOWNS ALOT
BUT SHE WOULD WIPE HER TEARS AND

GET BACK UP AND FIGHT AGAIN SO
KENEKA WENT OUT JOB SEARCHING THE
NEXT MORNING SHE WENT TO THE
WORRFORCE CENTER TO DO SOME
APPLICATIONS ON THE COMPUTER
KENEKA DID ABOUT 10 APPLICATIONS
THAT DAY SHE WAS MOTIVATED TO GET
WHAT SHE WANTED SO AFTER JOB
SEARCHING ALL DAY KENEKA HEADS
BACK HOME AND SHE CONTINUED TO AT
LEAST 10 APPLICATIONS PER DAY FOR
THAT WHOLE WEEK THE NEXT WEEK
KENEKA GETS A CALL FROM CHILLIS
TOO AT THE AIRPOT THEY ASK HER TO
COME IN FOR A INTERVIEW KENEKA
BEGANS TO SMILE AND SAYS YES I CAN

COME IN WHAT DAY WOULD YOU LIKE ME TO COME IN THEY LADY SAYS TOMORROW AT 11AM DOES THAT WORK FOR YOU KENEKA REPLIES YES THAT WILL WORK THEY LADY SAYS OK GREAT SEE YOU TOMORROW AT 11AM KENEKA REPLIES OK GREAT THANKS AND SHE HANGS UP THE PHONE KENEKA WAS SO EXCITED THE NEXT MORING KENEKA GOES IN WITH HER BEST INTERVIEW CLOTHES ON AND THEY GAVE HER ALL 3 INTERVIEWS AT ONE TIME THEN TOLD HER SHE WAS HIRED KENEKA WAS SO HAPPY SO SHE JUST HAD TO PASS HER DRUG SCREEN AND BACKGROUNG AND SHE WAS IN AND SHE KNEW SHE WOULD

PASS BOTH OF THEM SO SHE WAS TO
EXCITED THE NEXT WEEK THEY CALLED
HER BACK AND ASKED HER TO COME IN
THE NEXT MORNING KENEKA SAID OK ....
AND THE NEXT MORNING SHE WAS
THERE A HOUR EARLY SHE WASN'T
PLAYING ... HER FIRST DAY WENT GREAT
AND HER COWORKERS LOVED HER AND
ABOUT A COUPLE WEEKS AFTER SHE
GOT THE JOB WORKING AT CHILLIS TOO
IN THE AIRPORT SHE GOT A CALL FROM
A PLACE SHE PUT A APPLICATION IN AT
FOR A  APARTMENT  KENEKA WAS TO
HAPPY THEY ASKED HER TO COME IN
AND DO SOME PAPER WORK CAUSE HER
NAME CAME UP ON THE LIST SO SHE DID

HER PAPER WORK AND TOOK THE PAPER TO THE COUNTY TO HELP WITH THE DEPOSIT AND THE NEXT WEEK KENEKA HAD HER KEYS SHE WAS SO GREATFUL AND GLAD TO BE BACK IN HER OWN PLACE ONCE AGAIN KENEKA HELD DOWN HER JOB AND PLACE FOR 2 YEARS SHE WAS DOING REAL GOOD THIS TIME BUT THINGS TOOK A TURN FOR THE WORSE KENEKA WENT IN TO WORK AND HALF WAY THREW HER SHIFT ONE OF THE SERVERS CALL HE A NIGGER KENEKA TRYED TO KEEP HER COOL BUT SHE COULDNT KENEKA REPLIED WHAT YOU JUST CALL ME ????? I GOT YOUR NIGGER WAIT TILL ARE SHIFT IS OVER ...

THE GIRL WALKED AROUND LOOKING
SCARED AND SHE WAS RED IN THE FACE
ABOUT A HOUR LATTER TWO OTHER OF
KENEKAS COWORKERS SAME IN THAT
HOST WITH HER AT THE FRONT DOOR
AND THEY WHERE BOTH BLACK AS WELL
SO KENEKA TOLD THEM WHAT THE
SERVER CALLED HER AND THEY GOT
PISSED AND STARTED THREATING THE
SERVER AS WELL THEY WHERE REAL
COOL WITH KENEKA SO THEY WAS ON
HER SID ALL THE WAY THEN THEY BOTH
SAID TO HER WE GOING TO CATCH YOU
WHEN YOU GET OFF THE GIRL GOT
SUPER RED NEXT THING THEY KNEW SHE
CLOCKED OUT AND LEFT WAY BEFORE

HER SHIFT WAS OVER SHE QUIT HER JOB AND DIDNT NEVER COME BACK SHE WAS SCARED TO DEATH ... SHE LEFT BEFORE THE COULD GET TO HER THEY THOUGH SHE WAS JUST GOING ON BREAK BUT COME TO FIND OUT SHE WASNT SO THE NEXT DAY WHEN KENEKA COMES IN TO WORK SHE WAS TOLD THAT THEY HAD TO LET HER GO CAUSE SHE THREATED STAFF THEN KENEKA SAID WHY SHE CALLED ME A NIGGER WHAT YOU THINK SOMEONE IS GOING TO DO OR SAY WHEN THEY GET CALLED THAT , THATS FIGHTING WORDS KENEKAS MANGER SAID I UNDERSTAND BUT WE STILL HAVE TO LET YOU GO KENEKA WAS PISSED

KENEKA REPLIED OK AND SHE LEFT SO
KENEKA WENT HOME A GOT OUT OF HER
UNIFORM CLOTHES AND PUT HER DRESS
ON AND SOME FLIP FLOPS ON AND HIT
THE STREETS AGAIN SHE HAD TO FIND A
JOB QUICK SO SHE WOULDN'T LOOSE
HER PLACE SO KENEKA HEADS OUT TO
MALL OF AMERICA TO PUT IN SOME
APPLICATION IN KENEKA ALWAYS HAD
THE BEST OF LUCK GETTING ANOTHER
JOB FAST FOR SOME REASON SO AFTER
APPLYING AT ABOUT 8 PLACES INN THE
MALL KENEKA SEEN A SIGN ON THE
DRUGSTORE IN THE MALL OF AMERICA
THAT SAID NOW HIRING IMMEDIATELY
SO KENEKA STOPS IN THERE AND ASKED

FOR A APPLICATION AND FILLS IT OUT
RIGHT AWAY SHE GOES BACK TO THE
COUNTER AND ASK TO SPEAK TO THE
MANGER SO THE GIRL GOES AND GETS
THE MANGER FOR KENEKA  THE
MANGER COMES OUT AND SAYS HI MY
NAME IS HAROLD HOW MAY I HELP YOU
KENEKA REPLIES YES I JUST FINISHED
THE APPLICATION AND I WAS
WONDERING WHEN I CAN COME IN FOR A
INTERVIEW  HAROLD REPLISE WELL
LETS DO THE INTERVIEW RIGHT NOW
KENEKA LOOKS AT HIM WITH A
SURPRISED LOOK ON HER FACE AND
SAYS OK... SO HAROLD TAKES HER TO
THE BACK AND ASKED HER SOME

INTERVIEW QUESTIONS AND ONCE HE WAS DONE INTERVIEWING HER HE SAID TO KENEKA SO CAN YOU START TOMORROW AT 4PM AND WORK TILL CLOSES KENEKA WAS FILLED WITH JOY KENEKA REPLIES I SURE CAN HAROLD REPLIES OK GREAT ILL SEE YOU TOMORROW EVENING KENEKA REPLIES OK GREAT AND SHAKES HIS HAND AND SAYS THANK YOU SO MUCH AND ILL SEE YOU TOMORROW  KENEKA LEFT WITH A BIG SMILE ON HER FACES AND HEADS BACK HOME SHE ACCOMPLISED HER GOAL IN ONE DAY SHE STILL COULDN'T BELIEVE SHE GOT ANOTHER JOB THAT FAST... KENEKA THEN HEADS HOME AND

MAKES HER SELF SOME DINNER AND
WATCHES HER CABLE THE REST OF THE
NIGHT THE NEXT DAY SHE SHOWS UP AT
HER JOB 30 MINUTES EARLY SHE WAS SO
READY TO START HER SHIFT THE
MANGER REALLY LIKED KENEKA SO
AFTER A YEAR WORKING AT THE
DRUGSTORE THE MANGER APPROACHES
HER AND SAYS KENEKA YOU HAVE BEEN
DOING A REALLY GOOD JOB AND YOUR
ALWAYS ON TIME THEN KENEKA
REPLIES THANKYOU AND HAROLD
BEGANS TO SPEAK HE REPLISE YOUR
WELCOME THEN HAROLD SAYS TO
KENEKA I WANT TO MAKE YOU MY
ASSISTANCE MANGER KENEKA SAYS OUT

LOUD HUH….. WITH A SURPRISED LOOK ON HER FACE HAROLD LAUGHS AT KENEKAS RESPONSE AND SAYS IT AGAIN I WANT TO MAKE YOU MY ASSISTANT MANGER KENEKA REPLIES WITH A BIG SMILE ON HER FACE OK SURE … HAROLD REPLIES OK ARE YOU OK WITH WORKING THE MORNING SHIFT AND OPENING THE STORE IN THE MORNINGS KENEKA REPLIES YES …. I LIKE MORNING SHIFTS BETTER ANYWAY HAROLD REPLIES OK GREAT AND GIVES KENEKA THE KEYS TO OPEN THE STORE THE NEXT MORNING SO KENEKA FIINSHED HER SHIFT FOR THAT DAY AND LEFT AT 10PM SHE WENT HOME AND

WENT STRAIGHT TO BED CAUSE SHE HAD TO OPEN THE STORE FIRST THING IN THE MORNING IT WAS HARD FOR KENEKA TO GET TO SLEEP SHE COULD NOT BELIEVE SHE WAS PROMOTED TO ASSISTANT MANGER AND HAD KEYS TO THE STORE BUT EVENTUALLY SHE FELL A SLEEP THE NEXT MORNING KENEKA WAS UP AND MOVING SHE GOT TO WORK AT 8AM TO GET THE STORE READY TO OPEN KENEKA CONTINUED TO WORK THIS JOB FOR 4 YEARS STRAIGHT THEN THINGS TOOK A TURN FOR THE WORSE ONCE AGAIN KENEKAS MANGER CAN TO HER TO GIVE HER A HEADS UP THAT THE STORE WAS GOING OUT OF BUSINESS IN 1

MONTH KENEKA GOT VERY DEPRESSED AND DIDN'T KNOW WHAT SHE WAS GOING TO DO AFTER SHE GOT THE NEWS SHE WENT HOME THAT EVENING AND SHE RAN INTO HER FRIEND DC ON HER WAY UP TO HER APARTMENT DC STAYED IN THE SAME BUILDING AS KENEKA  DC SEEN THAT KENEKA WAS CRYING DC SAID TO KENEKA WHATS WRONG BABY GIRL KENEKA STARTED CRY ALL OVER AGAIN DC PUT HIS ARMS AROUND HER AND SAID COME UP TO MY APARTMENT WITH ME SO WE CAN TALK KENEKA REPLIED OK... WHEN THEY GOT BACK UP TO THE APARTMENT KENEKA SAT ON THE COUCH DC WENT TO GET HER SOME

TISSUE AND SAT NEXT TO HER AND SAID NOW WHATS GOING ON BABY GIRL KENEKA REPLIED MY JOB IS GOING OUT OF BUSINESS SO NOW I AM AT RISK OF LOSING MY PLACE IF I DONT FIND WORK SOON DC REPLIED OK WELL ILL TELL YOU WHAT I AM GETTING READY TO MOVE INTO A 2 BEDROOM DUPLEX SO IF YOU GET PUT OUT I GOT YOU BABY GIRL KENEKA REPLIED YOU DONT HAVE TO DO THAT ... DC REPLIED LOOK BABY GIRL I I KNOW YOU ARE VERY INDEPENDENT AND YOUR USE TO DOING EVERYTHING ON YOUR OWN BUT EVERYONE NEEDS A LITTLE HELP SOME TIMES .... HE WAS RIGHT KENEKA BEEN

DOING THINGS ON HER OWN SINCE SHE WAS 15 YEARS OLD SHE GREW UP FAST AND WAS VERY INDEPENDENT BUT KENEKA THOUGHT ABOUT IT FOR A MINUTE AND THEN KENEKA REPLIED OK .... THANKYOU DC DC REPLIED YOUR WELCOME AND HE ASKED KENEKA DO YOU KNOW HOW TO DRIVE KENEKA REPLIED YES .. DC REPLIED OK WELL I WORK OVER NIGHTS AND ONCE I GET OFF ALL I DO IS COME HOME AND SLEEP SO YOU CAN START TAKING MY CAR TO JOB SEARCH CAUSE I KNOW IT WILL BE FASTER THAN TRYING TO GO EVERY WHERE ON THE BUS ... KENEKA SAID HUH ARE YOU SERIOUS DC REPLIED YES ...

KENEKA REPLIED OH MY GOD THANK YOU SO MUCH AND HUGGED HIM DC REPLIED YOUR WELCOME BABY GIRL DC HANDED HER HIS KEYS AND SAID I AM ABOUT TO GO TO SLEEP NOW CAUSE I GOTTA WORK TONIGHT SO HAVE THE CAR BACK BY 10PM KENEKA REPLIED OK... ILL LET YOU GET SOME REST NOW I AM GOING TO GO CHANGED AND GET OUT HER AND APPLY AT PLACES DC REPLIED OK BABY GIRL ... AND KENEKA WALKED OUT THE DOOR SHE WENT BACK DOWN TO HER APARTMENT AND CHANGED INTO ONE OF HER SUMMER DRESSES AND GOT CUTE AND SHE HIT THE STREETS KENEKA WENT DOWN TO

THE PARKING LOT AND GOT IN THE CAR
KENEKA COULD NOT BELIEVE HE LET
HER HAVE THE CAR SHE WAS STILL IN
SHOCK BEFORE KENEKA COULD PULL
OFF KENEKA GETS A TEXT FROM BJ IT
SAID I WANT YOU BACK WHERE YOU AT
RIGHT NOW KENEKA REPLIED IM GOOD
NOT INTERESTED IN GETTING BACK
WITH YOU ... BJ REPLISE I WILL GET YOU
BACK AND ILL FIND YOU ONE WAY OR
THE OTHER KENEKA JUST LOOKED AT
HER PHONE AND DIDN'T REPLY SHE
DIDN'T KNOW WHY HE WAS TRYING TO
COME BACK IN HER LIFE AFTER HOW HE
TREATED HER SHE WAS TIRED OF HIM...
SO KENEKA THROWS THE PHONE DOWN

IN THE SEAT AND STARTS DRIVING
KENEKA HIT AS MANY PLACES AS SHE
COULD BEFORE DC NEEDED THE CAR
BACK TO GO TO WORK BUT KENEKA WAS
IN FOR A SURPRISE AFTER SHE PUT HER
APPLACATION IN AT RAINBOW FOODS
SHE WENT BACK TO GET IN THE CAR AS
SHE WAS WALKING TO THE CAR SHE SHE
HEARD A MAN SCREAM KENEKA !!!! SHE
RECOGNIZED THE VOICE AND TURNED
AROUND AND LOOKED IT WAS BJ
WALKING THREW THE PARKING LOT
KENEKA PUT UP HER MIDDLE FINGER
AND GOT BACK IN THE CAR BJ YELLED
SO YOU GOT SOME MANS CAR HUH
KENEKA PUT UP HER MIDDLE FINGER

AND STARTED THE CAR UP AND TOOK
OFF REAL FAST BEFORE BJ COULD MAKE
IT TO HER SHE WAS GONE.... NEXT THING
KENEKA KNEW HER PHONE WAS
RINGING IT WAS BJ BLOWING HER UP
AND HE WOULDN'T STOP CALLING HER
SO KENEKA TURNED HER PHONE OFF
AND CONTINUED ON HER JOB SEARCH
KENEKA DIDN'T WANT TO BE BOTHER
WITH BJ ANYMORE SHE WAS FOCUSED
ON HER JOB SEARCH AND WHAT SHE
NEEDED TO GET DONE KENEKA LOOKED
AT THE TIME IT WAS NOW 8PM SO
KENEKA STOPPED AT WHITE CASTLES
AND GOT HER SOME BURGERS AND WENT
TO FILL THE GAS TANK BACK UP THEN

HEADED BACK TO THE HOUSE CAUSE DC HAD TO GOT TO WORK SOON ... SO SHE MAD SURE SHE GOT BACK EARLY ... KENEKA GOT BACK HOME CLOSE TO 9PM SHE WENT BACK UP TO DC APARTMENT TO GIVE HIM HIS KEYS KENEKA KNOCKED ON THE DOOR DC REPLIED WHO IS IT KENEKA REPLIED ITS ME DC SAID OK HERE I COME DC OPENS THE DOOR KENEKA HANDS HIM THE KEYS AND SAYS I FILLED THE TANK BACK UP TOO DC LOOKS AT HER IN SHOCK AND SAYS OH OK YOU KNOW YOU DIDNT HAVE TO DO THAT RIGHT KENEKA REPLISE BUT I AM DRIVING THE GAS OUT SO I WANTED TO PUT IT BACK DC

REPLISE OK BABY GIRL ILL BE HERE AROUND 8AM ILL BRING THE KEYS TO YOUR APARTMENT BEFORE I GO TO SLEEP KENEKA REPLIES OK... SEE YOU IN THE MORNING DC REPLIES OK THEN KENEKA HEADS BACK TO HER APARTMENT DOWN STAIRS KENEKA TRUNS ON THE TV AND TURNED HER PHONE BACK ON AND NEXT THING KENEKA KNOWS HER PHONE IS GOING OFF LIKE CRAZY SHE PICKS HER PHONE BACK UP AND SEES SHE HAS 20 NEW VOICEMAIL FROM BJ KENEKA SAYS TO HER SELF THIS MAN HAS LOST HIS MIND WHY IS HE TRYING TO GET ME BACK AND WHY IS HE STOKING ME ALL OF A

SUDDEN KENEKA WAS PISSED … KENEKA BEGAN S TO CHECK THE MESSAGES AS SHE IS CHECKING THE MESSAGES SHE GETS A INCOMING CALL FROM BJ KENEKA CUSSES AND ENDS THE CALL AND TURNS HER PHONE RIGHT BACK OFF FOR THE REST OF THE NIGHT …. THE NEXT DAY KENEKA GOES UP TO DC'S APARTMENT TO GET THE CAR KEYS SO SHE CAN GO OUT JOB SEARCHING KENEKA HITS THE MIDWAY MALL TO GO APPLY AT SOME STORES IN THE MIDWAY AND KENEKA SEES THIS TRUCK THAT HAS A BILLBOARD ON IT  KENEKA GOES OVER TO THE MAN THAT WAS SITTING IN THE TRUCK AND ASKED HIM IF THE

COMPANY IS HIRING FOR DRIVERS THE MAN REPLIES YES WE ARE I HAVE A APPLICATION IN MY TURCK THE MAN HANDS KENEKA THE APPLICATION AND TELLS HER TO FILL IT OUT NOW AND HE CAN SEND IT IN TO HIS BOSS RIGHT AWAY KENEKA REPLIES OK GREAT AND SHE GOES BACK TO SIT IN THE CAR TO FILL OUT THE APPLICATION THEN WHEN KENEKA GOES BACK TO THE TRUCK TO HAND IT BACK TO THE MAN HE TELLS HER HE JUST GOT OFF THE PHONE WITH THE HIRING MANGER AND HE WANTS HER TO START RIGHT AWAY KENEKA WAS SHOCKED KENEKA REPLIED OK GREAT THE MAN REPLIES CAN YOU MEET

ME HERE TOMORROW AT 10AM SO WE CAN GET A COPY OF YOUR DRIVERS LICENSE AND SSN# AND FAX IT IN SO WE CAN GET YOU ON PAY ROLL  AND GET YOU STARTED WITH YOUR TRAINING KENEKA REPLIES YES I CAN MEET YOU HERE AT 10AM TOMORROW MORNING THAT MAN REPLIES OK GREAT ILL SEE YOU TOMORROW AT 10AM KENEKA REPLIES OK GREAT THANKS AND HEADS BACK TO THE CAR KENEKA GOT LUCK ONCE AGAIN WITH FINDING A JOB FAST SHE COULDN'T BELIEVE IT … SO KENEKA DIDNT KNOW WHAT ELSE TO DO HER JOB SEARCH WAS COMPLETED FOR THE DAY SO KENEKA DESIDES TO GO JOY RIDING

FOR A LITTLE BIT SO SHE TURNS UP THE
RADIO AND HER SONG WAS ON SHE
STARTS SINGING I.N.D.E.P.E.N.D.E.N.T DO
YOU KNOW WHAT THAT MEAN MAN SHE
GOT HER OWN HOUSE SHE GOT HER OWN
CAR ..... SHES DANCING AND SINGING
WHILE DRIVING PEOPLE WAS LOOKING
AT HER AND SMILING KENEKA DIDNT
CARE SHE WAS JAMMING  KENEKA WAS
SO HAPPY SHE GOT ANOTHER JOB SO ON
HER WAY DOWN UNIVERSITY AVE
KENEKA SEES BLACK DRESSED IN HIS
FAVORITE COLOR RED SO KENEKA PULLS
OVER AND HONKS THE HORN BLACK
STARTS LOOKING AT THE CAR WHILE
HES WAITING FOR THE BUS AT THE BUS

STOP KENEKA YELLS IT ME KENEKA
BLACK STARTS WALKING TO THE CAR
STILL UN SURE WHO IT WAS THEN WHEN
BLACK GETS TO THE WINDOW HE SAYS
OH WHATS UP I DIDN'T KNOW YOU
WHERE DRIVING KENEKA REPLIES NO
THIS IS MY FRIENDS CAR THEY TALK FOR
A COUPLE SECONDS AND BLACK SAYS I
HAVE TO GO NOW I AM IN THE MIDDLE
OF TAKING CARE OF SOMETHING
KENEKA REPLIES OK SEE YOU AROUND
AND KENEKA PULLS OFF KENEKA TURNS
HER RADIO BACK UP AND SHE STARTS TO
GET IN HER FEELINGS BIG TIME SHE
LOVED BLACK SO MUCH AND WANTED
HIM SO BAD BUT SHE COULD NOT HAVE

HIM KENEKA WAS SO IN LOVE WITH BLACK BUT HE JUST WOULDN'T DO RIGHT BY HER KENEKA GOT TO REMINISCING ABOUT THE GOOD TIMES SHE HAD WITH BLACK BACK IN THE DAY AND TEARS BEGAN TO FALL FROM HER EYES SHE BEGAN S TO THINK TO HER SELF WHY DO I ALWAYS GET DOGGED BY MEN I AM FAITHFUL AND HONEST AND I AM WIFEY MATERIAL BUT SEEMS LIKE MEN JUST CANT SEE THAT ... KENEKA WIPES HER TEARS AND DESIDES SHE IS GOING TO STOP AT HER MOMS HOUSE TO SEE HER LITTLE BROTHER AND SISTER ABOUT 5 MINTURES LATER KENEKA PULLS INTO THE DRIVE WAY AND HER

MOM SEEN HER PULL UP SO HER MOM
OPENS THE DOOR AND SAID YOU DRIVING
HOWS CAR IS THAT KENEKA STARTS
LAUGHING AND REPLIES ITS MY FRIEND
DC'S CAR HE LETS ME USE THE CAR
DURING THE DAY KENEKAS MOM
REPLIES OH OK KENEKA GOES IN THE
HOUSE SHE STAYED FOR ABOUT A HOUR
THEN SHE LEAVES SHE WENT TO GO SIT
AT ONE OF HER FAVORITE LAKES AND
SHE BEGAN TO JUST THINK ABOUT HER
LIFE AND THINGS SHE HAS BEEN THREW
AND KENEKA COULD NOT GET BLACK
OFF HER MIND SINCE SEE SEEN HIM
EARLY THAT DAY HER FEELINGS WHERE
REAL DEEP FAR A BLACK GOES SHE

WANTED TO SPEND THE REST OF HER LIFE WITH BLACK AND BE HIS WIFE BUT HEY WHAT CAN YOU SAY YOU DON'T ALWAYS GET WHAT YOU WANT IN LIFE THAT'S LIFE FOR YOU KENEKA BEGAN TO THINK TO HER SELF KENEKAS PHONE BEGAN TO RINGING SHE LOOKS TO SEE WHO IT WAS ... SHE LOOKED AT THE PHONE AND CUSSED IT WAS BJ TRYING TO GET BACK WITH KENEKA ONCE AGAIN KENEKA DIDN'T ANSWER IT WAS GETTING CLOSER TO THE TIME TO BRING THE CAR BACK SO KENEKA STARED UP THE CAR AND HEADED HOME ... KENEKA PULLED IN TO THE PARKING LOT AND PARKED THE CAR THEN

HEADED UP STAIRS TO BRING DC THE KEYS AND TELL HIM THE GOOD NEWS KENEKA BEGAN TO KNOCK ON THE DOOR DC SAID WHO IS IT KENEKA REPLIED ITS ME DC OPENS THE DOOR AND SAYS SOME IN KENEKA WALKS IN AND SITS ON THE COUCH DC ASKS SO HOW DID IT GO KENEKA REPLIED GREAT I GOT A JOB !!! DC REPLIES WHAT !!! WHERE ??? KENEKA REPLIES ITS A COMPANY CALLED DO IT OUT DOORS THEY DRIVE AROUND WITH MOBILE BILLBOARDS ON THE TRUCK AND ADVERTISE FOR DIFFERENT COMPANY'S DC REPLIES WOW OK THAT'S GREAT WHEN DO YOU START KENEKA REPLIES

TOMORROW AT 10AM BUT I DON'T WANNA TAKE YOUR CAR ILL JUST CATCH THE BUS CAUSE I DON'T KNOW WHAT TIME I WILL GET DONE AND I DON'T WANNA MAKE YOU LATE FOR WORK DC REPLIES OK THAT'S COOL KENEKA REPLIES I AM GOING TO GO DOWNSTAIRS NOW TO GET SOME REST DC REPLIES OK I AM PROUD OF YOU CONGRATULATIONS ON THE NEW JOB KENEKA REPLIES THANKS AND HEADS BACK DOWN STAIRS TO HER APARTMENT ASK KENEKA LAID DOWN SHE HAD BLACK ON HER MIND REAL TOUGH TO THE POINT IT WAS HARD FOR HER TO GET TO SLEEP SHE TOSSED AND TURNED FOR A COUPLE

HOURS THEN FINALLY FELL A SLEEP THE NEXT MORNING KENEKA GOT UP AND GOT READY FOR WORK AND HEADED TO THE BUS STOP TO GET THE BUS TO GO TO MIDWAY KENEKA ARRIVED AT MIDWAY AT ABOUT 9:45AM THE MAN WAS SITTING IN THE PARKING LOT WAITING FOR HER TO GET THERE ALREADY SO KENEKA WALKS TO THE TRUCK THE MAN SAYS HEY GOOD MORNING KENEKA REPLIES GOOD MORNING THE MAN TELLS KENEKA TO JUMP IN THE OTHER SIDE OF THE TRUCK SO KENEKA JUMPS IN THEY GO TO GET COPYS OF HER SSN# AND DRIVERS LICENSE THEN KENEKA BEGAN HER

TRAINING BEHIND THE WHEEL OF THE TRUCK KENEKA WAS DOING GOOD BUT WHEN SHE HAD TO STOP AT THE LIGHT SHE HIT THE BREAKS AND THE WHOLE TRUCK JERKED BOTH OF THEN KENEKA LOOKS AT THE MAN AND SAYS WHY DID IT DO THAT I BARELY TOUCHED THE BREAK THE MAN BEGAN TO LAUGH KENEKA JUST LOOKS AT HIM … THE MAN REPLIES YOU HAVEN'T DROVE WITH AIR BRAKES BEFORE HUH KENEKA REPLIES NO. THE MAN LAUGHS AGAIN KENEKA STARTS LAUGHING TO THE MAN REPLIES THEY ARE NOT LIKE NORMAL BREAKS ON A CAR BUT YOU JUST GOTTA GET USE TO THEM YOU WILL GET IT AFTER A

WHILE DON'T WORRY ABOUT IT KENEKA REPLIES OH OK AND CONTINUES DRIVING AFTER A COUPLE HOURS BEHIND THE WHEEL KENEKA HAD LEARNED HOW TO WORK WITH THE AIR BREAKS AND SHE DID GOOD FOR THE REST OF HER TRAINING DAY  KENEKA DID A FULL WEEK OF TRAINING AND THE FOLLOWING WEEK SHE WAS ONE HER OWN KENEKA WAS LOVING THIS JOB SHE GOT PAID JUST TO DRIVE AROUND ALL DAY IN DIFFERENT AREAS AND KENEKA LOVED DRIVING KENEKA WAS INTO WORKING HER SECOND WEEK BY HER SELF AND SHE WAS TOLD TO SIT AT DIFFERENT MALLS FOR THE DAY SO

KENEKA SAT AT MIDWAY MALL IN THE CUBS PARKING LOT FOR A COUPLE HOURS AFTER THE SECOND HOUR INTO HER SHIFT SHE STARTED GETTING HUNGRY SO KENEKA WENT IN TO CUB FOOD TO GET SOME FRIED CHICKEN AND A MOUNTAIN DEW AFTER PAYING FOR HER THINGS KENEKA PROCEEDED BACK TO HER TRUCK AS KENEKA WALKS BACK TO THE TRUCK SHE HERES HEY KENEKA !!!! KENEKA CUSSES CAUSE SHE KNOWS THAT VOICE KENEKA STOPS AND TURNS AROUND IT WAS BJ ONCE AGAIN KENEKA STICKS UP HER MIDDLE FINGER AND TURNS AROUND AND WALKS TO THE TRUCK VERY FAST SHE TURNS TO LOOK

BEHIND HER AND SHES HIM HEADING TOWARDS HER KENEKA STARTS RUNNING SHE OPENS THE TRUCK VERY FAST AND GETS IN AND LOCKS ALL THE DOORS SO HE CANT GET IN THE TRUCK KENEKA COULDN'T LEAVE QUITE YET SHE HAD TO SIT THERE FOR ANOTHER 30 MINTUES BEFORE SHE COULD MOVE THE TRUCK TO A DIFFERENT MALL SOON AS BJ GETS TO THE TRUCK HE TRYS TO OPEN THE DOOR AND SEES ITS LOCKED THEN BJ JUMPED ON THE TRUCK HOLDING TO THE BAR YOU GRAB TO CLIMB INTO THE TRUCK AND BJ BEGANS TO SAY KENEKA OPEN THIS DOOR KENEKA STICKS HER FINGER UP AGAIN

BJ BEGINS TO YELL KENEKA OPEN THIS DOOR NOW!!! KENEKA CUSSES AT HIM AND TELLS HIM TO GET OFF THE COMPANY TRUCK BEFORE SHE CALLS THE POLICE BJ LOOKS AT HER WITH A EVIL LOOK IN HIS EYES AND GETS OFF THE TRUCK BJ BEGAN TO WALK AROUND TO HER SIDE KENEKA HAD THE WINDOW CRACKED JUST A TINNY BIT SHE MADE SURE BJ COULD NOT TRY TO GET IN BY PUTTING HIS HAND THREW THE WINDOW BJ BEGINS TO SPEAK WHY YOU DOING ME LIKE THIS AND NOT ANSWERING MY CALLS KENEKA RESPONDS DUDE WE AIN'T TOGETHER NO MORE SO WHY YOU KEEP HARASSING ME !!!! BJ RESPONDS

BECAUSE I WANT YOU BACK AND I AM
SORRY FOR HOW I TREATED YOU
KENEKA CUSSES I DIDN'T REALLY WANT
YOU ANYWAY I REALLY WANT BLACK
BACK BJ LOOKS AT HER WITH A EVIL
LOOK ON HIS FACE BJ REPLY S YEAH OK
LIKE I SAID I WANT YOU BACK KENEKA
LOOKS AT THE TIME AND SEES SHE IS
ABLE TO MOVE THE TRUCK TO A NEW
LOCATION NOW SO KENEKA TELLS BJ ITS
TIME FOR ME TO DRIVE AGAIN AND
STARTS UP THE TRUCK AND PUTS IT INTO
DRIVE BJ YELLS DID YOU HEAR WHAT I
SAID KENEKA STICKS UP HER MIDDLE
FINGER AND BEGAN TO MOVE THE
TRUCK BJ TRYS TO GET IN HER WAY SO

SHE CANT MOVE THE TRUCK KENEKA
YELLS YOU BETTER GET OUT MY WAY
FOR I RUN YOU OVER BJ KEEPS
STANDING THERE LIKE KENEKA
WOULDN'T DO IT BUT KENEKA KEPT
MOVING THE TRUCK SLOWY ANYWAY  BJ
LOOKED AT HER WITH SHOCK AND
YELLED OH SO YOU TRYING TO KILL ME
NOW KENEKA YELLS BACK GET YOUR
BUTT OUT THE WAY YOU TRYING TO
KILL YOUR SELF BY STANDING BY A
MOVING TRUCK BJ JUMPS OUT THE WAY
AFTER SEEING KENEKA WASN'T PLAYING
AS KENEKA PULLS OFF BJ YELLS ILL FIND
YOU AGAIN YOU CANT HIDE THIS BIG
TURCK AS KENEKA IS DRIVING OFF SHE

ROLLS DOWN THE WINDOW AND STICKS UP HER MIDDLE FINGER AGAIN AT BJ AND CONTINUES WITH THE REST OF HER SHIFT … KENEKA RETURNS BACK HOME THAT EVENING AND DC CALLS HER AND ASK HER TO STOP UP STAIRS FOR A MINUTE KENEKA SAYS OK AND HEADS UP STAIRS KENEKA KNOCKS ON THE DOOR AND DC SAYS COME ON IN ITS OPEN SO KENEKA WALKS IN AND SITS ON THE COUCH DC BEGANS TO TALK YOU KNOW I AM MOVING IN 2 DAYS I GOT THE PLACE AND I WAS JUST CHECKING WITH YOU TO SEE IF YOU WANT TO MOVE WITH ME KENEKA LOOKS AT DC THEN RELPIES YEAH WHY NOT PLUS I DONT REALLY

HAVE NO WHERE TO PARK THE TRUCK HERE AFTER MY SHIFT BECAUSE THE WHOLE STREET IS NO PARKING SO I HAVE BEEN PARKING IT A COUPLE BLOCKS OVER DC REPLIES OK GREAT AND YEAH YOU GOT A POINT SO YOU SURE YOU WANT TO MOVE DONT FEEL LIKE YOU HAVE TO CAUSE I ASKED YOU KENEKA REPLIES NO NO NO I AM SURE THEY MIGHT TRY TO PUT A UD ON ME CAUSE I AM A MONTH BEHIND FROM WHEN I LOST THE LAST JOB SO ILL JUST MOVE OUT NOW BEFORE THEY PUT ONE ON ME DC REPLIES OK COOL SO ILL GET A COPY MADE OF THE KEYS AND SHOW YOU WHERE IT IS ONCE I GET ALL

MOVED IN KENEKA REPLIES OK GREAT
KENEKA THEN HEADS BACK DOWN TO
HER ROOM  TO GET SOME REST THE
NEXT MORNING KENEKA GETS UP AND
GOES TO WORK AND SHE CONTINUES TO
WORK HER SHIFTS EACH DAY ON TIME 2
DAYS LATER DC CALLS KENEKA WHILE
SHES OUT DRIVING THE TRUCK DC SAYS
HEY I JUST GOT DONE MOVING IN THE
DUPLEX AND GIVES HER THE ADDRESS
AND TELLS HER TO COME ON OVER TO
GET HER KEY AND SEE THE PLACE SO
KENEKA REPLIES OK IM ON MY WAY
WHEN KENEKA ARRIVES THE FIRST
THING SHE NOTICES IS THERE IS PLENTY
OF ROOM FOR HER TO PARK HER WORK

TRUCK RIGHT BY THE HOUSE AND THE STREET WAS NOT LIMITED ON PARKING SHE WAS HAPPY ABOUT THAT KENEKA PARKS THE TRUCK AND JUMPS OUT DC WAS AT THE DOOR WAITING FOR HER TO ARRIVE KENEKA GETS TO THE STOP OF THE STAIRS AND DC SAYS HEY HERES YOUR KEYS KENEKA REPLIES THANKS AND THEY GO IN AND HE SHOWS HER THE PLACE KENEKA LOVES IT AND HER AND DC BOTH HAD THERE OWN ROOM SO AFTER HER SHIFT WAS OVER SHE PARKS HER TRUCK AT THE NEW HOUSE AND DC GIVES HER THE CAR SO SHE CAN GO GET HER STUFF FROM THE OTHER PLACE SHE GETS EVERYTHING PACKED AND LOADED

INTO THE CAR WHEN SHE GETS BACK TO DC S HE HELPS HER BRING EVERYTHING IN THEN DC STARTS GETTING READY FOR WORK KENEKA WAS GLAD TO HAVE A BIGGER PLACE CAUSE SHE JUST HAD A ROOM AT THE OTHER PLACE AND SO DID DC SO THEY WHERE BOTH HAPPY ABOUT THE NEW PLACE TWO WEEKS LATER THINGS WHERE STILL GOING GREAT AND KENEKA STILL HAD HER JOB AND WAS DOING WELL LATER THAT EVENING KENEKA PARKS THE TRUCK BACK AT THE HOUSE DC AND KENEKA WHERE JUST RELAXING WATCHING TV KENEKA WAS SUPRISED THAT DC WAS REALLY NOT TRYING TO COME ON TO HER SHE

WAS THINKING HE WAS TRYING TO GET WITH HER BUT DC WASNT ON THAT HE KNEW WHAT A FRIEND MET AND HE DID CROSS THAT BOUNDARY WITH KENEKA AT ALL ABOUT A HOUR LATER KENEKA AND DC ARE WATCHING MOVES STILL CAUSE DC HAD THE NIGHT OFF AND ALL OF A SUDDEN KENEKA HEARS A VOICE YELL KENEKA !!!! KENEKA CUSSES DC REPLIES WHATS WRONG KENEKA REPLISE THATS MY EX HES BEEN STOCKING ME AND TRYING TO GET ME BACK ... BJ YELLS AGAIN KENEKA !!!! I KNOW YOU IN THERE YOU CANT HIDE FROM ME NOW I SEE YOUR WORK TRUCK OUT HERE SO I KNOW YOU HERE DC

JUMPS UP AND GOES TO THE WINDOW AND SAYS DONT COME OVER HERE WITH ALL THAT YELLING BJ CUSSES AT HIM AND SAYS WHO ARE YOU HER MAN DC REPLIES NO I AM HER FRIEND BUT WHY YOU WORRIED ABOUT HOW SHE WITH SHE AINT WITH YOU RIGHT NOW ANYWAY BJ CUSSES AND TELLS DC MIND HIS OWN BUSINESS DC REPLIES IT IS MY BUSINESS WHEN YOU COME TO MY HOUSE YELLING LIKE YOU LOST YOUR MIND BJ REPLIES LOOK I JUST WANNA TALK TO KENEKA DC REPLIES KENEKA IS SLEEP RIGHT NOW AND I AIN'T WAKING HER UP BJ REPLIES YEAH OK AND HE LEAVES KENEKA COMES BACK OUT

FROM THE BACK ROOM AND DC SAYS WHY DIDNT YOU TELL ME YOUR EX WAS STOCKING YOU KENEKA REPLIES I DIDN'T THINK HE WOULD FIND ME BUT HE DID BECAUSE OF THAT TRUCK I DRIVE IT STICKS OUT LIKE A SORE THUMB  AND I DIDNT EXPECT HIM TO FIND ME OVER ON THIS SIDE OF TOWN BUT HE HAS BEEN POPIN UP OUT OF NO WHERE EVEN WHEN I AM OUT IN THE STREETS HE WONT LEAVE ME ALONE AND HES REALLY TRYING TO GET ME BACK DC REPLISE OK I AIN'T WORRIED ABOUT IT CAUSE WHERE JUST FRIENDS BUT I STILL AIN'T GOING TO LET HIM DO NOTHING TO YOU I WILL GO TO JAIL I AIN'T SCARED OF NO

MAN KENEKA REPLIES OK AND THANKS
FOR LOOKING OUT FOR ME I
APPRECIATE IT DC REPLIES NO PROBLEM
I AM JUST GLAD I WAS HERE AND NOT AT
WORK KENEKA REPLIES ME TO BUT I
DONT WANT YOU TO GO TO JAIL
BECAUSE OF ME AND LOSE YOUR JOB I
GOT HIM DC REPLIES I HEAR WHAT YOU
SAYING BUT HE AIN'T GOING TO BE ON
THAT IN FRONT OF ME KENEKA REPLIES
OK DC  AND THEY CONTINUE WATCHING
THE MOVE ON TV  ABOUT A HOUR LATER
KENEKAS EYES START GETTING HEAVY
SHE WAS GETTING TIRED SO SHE SAYS TO
DC I CANT HANG ANY LONGER I AM
SLEEPY SO I AM GOING TO BED DC

REPLIES OK GOOD NIGHT SEE YOU IN THE MORNING KENEKA REPLIES GOODNIGHT THE NEXT MORNING KENEKA GETS UP AND GETS READY TO JUMP IN THE TRUCK TO START HER SHIFT WHILE KENEKA WAS OUT DRIVING AROUND SHE SEES A PLACE FOR RENT KENEKA STOPS AND PUTS THE NUMBER IN HER PHONE KENEKA CALLS WHILE SHE IS STILL SITTING THERE SHE GETS NO ANSWER SO SHE LEAVES A MESSAGE KENEKA WANTED TO GET HER OWN PLACE BECAUSE SHE DIDN'T WANT DC TO END UP GOING TO JAIL BECAUSE OF HER AND SHE SEES THAT BJ JUST AIN'T TRYING TO LEAVE HER ALONE SO SHE

WANTS TO MOVE ASAP CAUSE SHE FEELS GUILTY ABOUT DC NOW BEING INVOLVED WITH WHAT SHE HAS GOING ON DC IS DOING GOOD AND SHE DON'T WANT TO SEE HIM MESS THAT UP BECAUSE OF HER SO SHE LEAVES A MESSAGE ON THE VOICE MAIL AND CONTINUES WITH HER DRIVING THEN AT THE END OF HER SHIFT KENEKA HEADS HOME TO PARK THE TRUCK ABOUT 2 WEEKS LATER KENEKA GETS A CALL BACK FROM THE APARTMENT SHE SEEN THAT WAS FOR RENT SHE WAS THINKING THEY WEREN'T RENTING IT ANYMORE CAUSE IT TOOK SO LONG FOR THEM TO GET BACK TO HER BUT KENEKA WAS

VERY HAPPY TO HEAR FROM THEM FINALLY THE LANDLORD ASK KENEKA WHEN SHE WAS AVAILABLE TO COME LOOK AT THE PLACE KENEKA REPLIED TOMORROW WILL WORK FOR ME AND THE LANDLORD SAID OK GREAT SEE YOU TOMORROW AT 11AM  KENEKA REPLIED OK GREAT SEE YOU IN THE MORNING KENEKA WAS SO EXCITED AND COULDN'T WAIT TILL THE MORNING KENEKA WAS GRATEFUL FOR DC'S HELP BUT SHE DIDN'T FEEL COMFORTABLE HAVING A MAN HELP HER GET THINGS DONE AND SHE ALSO SEEN BJ WAS NOT GOING TO LET UP AND SHE DIDN'T WANT DC TO BE IN THE MIDDLE OF WHAT WAS GOING ON

OR TO END UP IN JAIL BECAUSE OF HER

SO THE NEXT MORNING KENEKA WAS

THERE TO SEE THE PLACE AT 10:45 AM

THE LANDLORD PULLED UP ON THE

OPPOSITE SIDE OF THE STREET RIGHT AT

11AM  KENEKA JUMPS OUT THE TRUCK

AND WALKS TOWARDS HIM AND HE ASK

ARE YOU KENEKA     KENEKA REPLIES

YES I AM AND HE SAY OH OK IM BEN NICE

TO MEET YOU THEN BEN ASKS IS THAT

THE COMPANY YOU WORK FOR KENEKA

REPLIES YES THEN BEN REPLIES OK IS

THAT A BILLBOARD TRUCK KENEKA

REPLIES YES IT IS I DRIVE AROUND

ADVERTISING ALL DAY FOR DIFFERENT

COMPANY BEN REPLIES OH OK THAT'S A

GOOD JOB TO HAVE JUST DRIVING ALL DAY KENEKA REPLIES YES IT IS AND I LOVE IT ... BEN REPLIES OK THAT'S GOOD WELL I DON'T HAVE TO ASK YOU IF YOU HAVE A JOB I SEE THE TRUCK ALREADY THEY BOTH START LAUGHING THEN BEN SAYS OK LETS GO INSIDE SO YOU CAN SEE THE PLACE AND DO THE APPLICATION KENEKA REPILES OK AND FOLLOWS HIM IN SIDE WHEN THEY GET IN KENEKA GOES THREW EACH ROOM OF THE HOUSE AND THEN REPLIES I LIKE THIS ITS NICE BEN REPLIES OK GREAT BEN ASK KENEKA ABOUT HER RENTAL HISTORY AND A FEW OTHER QUESTIONS THEN HAS KENEKA FILL OUT THE

APPLICATION AND WHEN KENEKA IS DONE HE GIVES HER A PAPER TO TAKE TO THE COUNTY TO GET HER DEPOSIT PAID AND TELLS KENEKA AS SOON AS THE DEPOSIT KENEKA CAN MOVE IN KENEKA LOOKED AT HIM IN SHOCK ... AND REPLIED I GOT THE PLACE ? BEEN REPLIES YEAH YOU GOT IT KENEKA SAYS OK GREAT BEN REPLIES AS SOON AS I GET THE DEPOSIT AND FIRST MONTHS RENT I WILL CALL YOU TO COME GET YOUR KEYS KENEKA REPLIED OK GREAT AND SHE LEFT TO GO DOWN TO THE COUNTY TO GET HER APARTMENT PAID FOR ABOUT A WEEK LATER KENEKA GOT A CALL FROM BEN TELLING HER THAT

HE GOT EVERYTHING AND SHE COULD COME GET HER KEYS AND MOVE IN KENEKA REPLIED OK GREAT WHEN KENEKA HUNG UP THE PHONE SHE SCREAMED YES!!!!!!! I GOT THE PLACE !!!!! SHE WAS SO EXCITED AFTER HER SHIFT WAS OVER KENEKA WENT HOME AND PACKED HER STUFF UP AND USED HER TRUCK TO MOVE EVERYTHING TO HER PLACE CAUSE DC WAS AT WORK SO SHE COULDN'T USE THE CAR TO MOVE EVERYTHING OUT  ONCE EVERYTHING WAS PACKED AND LOADED KENEKA HEADED BACK TO HER PLACE AND UNLOADED EVERYTHING AND UN PACED AND THEN SHE RELAXED FOR THE REST

OF THE EVENING IN HER NEW PLACE
THE NEXT MORNING KENEKA GOT UP
FOR WORK AND JUMPED IN THE TRUCK
SHE WENT TO GIVE DC HIS KEYS BACK
WHEN KENEKA ARRIVED DC WAS JUST
GETTING HOME AND KENEKA SAID
HERE'S YOUR KEYS AND THANK YOU FOR
YOUR HELP  DC REPLIES HUH… WHATS
GOING ON KENEKA REPLIES I GOT MY
OWN PLACE NOW I DIDNT WANT YOU TO
HAVE TO DEAL WITH BJ COMING
AROUND YOUR HOUSE AND I DINT NEED
YOU GOING TO JAIL BECAUSE OF WHATS
GOING ON IN MY LIFE PLUS I AM USE TO
HAVING MY OWN AND DOING THINGS ON
MY OWN ITS NOTHING PERSONAL I AM

JUST VERY INDEPENDENT THATS ALL BEEN THAT WAY SINCE I WAS 15YEARS OLD I HAD TO GROW UP KINDA FAST AND IT CAUSED ME TO BECOME VERY INDEPENDENT DC REPLIES I KNOW .... I KNOW HOW YOU ARE BY NOW I GOT THE RENT ON MY OWN I WAS JUST SHOCK CAUSE I DIDN'T KNOW WHAT WAS GOING ON WHEN YOU HANDED ME THE KEYS BACK THAT'S ALL AND YOU RIGHT I WOULD OF PROBABLY WOULD OF ENDED UP IN JAIL CAUSE AIN'T NO MAN GOING TO BE DISRESPECTING YOU IN FRONT OF ME KENEKA REPLIES EXACTLY THAT'S WHY I HAD TO MAKE MOVES CAUSE HE AIN'T GOING TO STOP  DC REPLIES OK

WELL IF YOU NEED ME CALL ME I GOT YOU KENEKA REPLIES OK I WILL DC SAYS GIVE ME A HUG GIRL KENEKA HUGS HIM WHILE DC IS HUGGING HER HE SAYS I AM VERY CONCERNED ABOUT YOUR SAFETY SO PLEASE CALL ME IF THINGS GET OUT OF HAND AND YOU NEED HELP KENEKA SAYS OK DC I WILL BUT I CAN TAKE BJ I KNOCKED HIM OUT TWICE WITH ONE HIT DC LAUGHS HARD KENEKA STARTS LAUGHING TO AND DC SAYS OK BUT STILL IF YOU NEED ME YOU KNOW WHERE I AM AT AND YOU GOT MY NUMBER KENEKA REPLIES OK WELL I GOTTA GET BACK TO WORK ILL TALK TO YOU LATER DC REPLIES OK

SWEETHEART SEE YOU LATER TAKE
CARE KENEKA HEADS BACK TO HER
TRUCK TO FINNISH WORKING FOR THE
NEXT 2 MONTHS KENEKA WAS DOING
SHE STILL HAD HER JOB AND PLACE
KENEKA WAS OUT ON HER ROUTE AND
SHE RUNS INTO BLACK AGAIN THEY
TALK FOR A LITTLE BIT BLACK ASK HER
WHERE SHE WAS STAYING AT AND GAVE
HIM HER PHONE NUMBER THEN KENEKA
WENT BACK TO DRIVING HER ROUITE
THEN WHEN KENEKA GOT DONE WITH
HER SHIFT THAT EVENING SHE GOT A
CALL FROM BLACK , BLACK WAS ASKING
HER IF HIS COUSIN GREG COULD STAY AT
HER HOUSE FOR THE NIGHT CAUSE HE

WAS TO DRUNK TO KEEP DRIVING HIS CAR AND KENEKA REPLIED OK SURE AND GAVE BLACK THE ADDRESS SO HE COULD BRING HIM OVER ABOUT 30 MINTUES LATER BLACK ARIVES AT HER HOUSE KENEKA OPENS THE DOOR AND SAYS HEY COME ON IN KENEKA AND BLACK TALK FOR A MINUTE THEN BLACK TELLS KENEKA HE WAS ABOUT TO GO KENEKA REPLIED WAIT WHAT SO YOU JUST GOING TO LEAVE YOUR COUISIN HERE AND YOU AINT STAYING HER WITH HIM BLACK REPLIES I CANT STAY I GOT SOME OTHER STUFF TO HANDLE KENEKA REPLIES OK THEN BLACK LEAVES KENEKA THOUGHT HER AND BLACK

WOULD END UP BACK TOGETER SINCE THEY WHERE TALKING AGAIN BUT IT DIDN'T HAPPEN A HOUR LATER KENEKA GOES TO BED BUT KENEKA REALLY DIDN'T FEEL COMFORTABLE WITH GREG STAYING THERE CAUSE SHE DIDN'T KNOW HIM DO IT WAS HARD FOR HER TO EVEN GET TO SLEEP AFTER TOSSING AND TURNING FOR A COUPLE HOURS KENEKA FEEL A SLEEP FINALLY THE NEXT MORNING KENEKA GETS UP AND GOES IN THE LIVING ROOM AND DOESNT SEE GREG LAYING ON THE COUCH ANYMORE SHE SAYS GREG OUT LOUD ARE YOU STILL HERE BUT NO ANSWER SO SHE BEGANS TO CHECK EVERY ROOM IN HER

HOUSE BUT SHE DIDNT SEE HIM SHE
LOOKS AT THE DOOR AND SEES ITS UN
LOCKED  SO GREG LEFT BEFORE SHE
WOKE UP SO KENEKA LOCKS HER DOOR
AND STARTS GETTING READY FOR WORK
ABOUT TWO WEEKS PAST KENEKA WAS
JUST PARKING HER TRUCK AND GOES IN
THE HOUSE TO MAKE HER SELF SOME
DINNER AS SHE IS SITTING DOWN
WATCHING TV AND EATING KENEKA
HEARS A MAN YELLING THE MAN WAS
YELLING KENEKA !!!! SHE KNEW THAT
VOICE AND KENEKA CUSSED AND SAID
HOW DID HE FIND ME AGAIN THAT
TRUCK I ALL READY KNOW BJ YELLS
AGAIN KENEKA !!!! SO KENEKA GOES TO

HER WINDOW AND PEAKS OUT BJ WAS STANDING ON HER POURCH SO KENEKA GOES TO THE DOOR SO HE WILL STOP YELLING AND DRAWING ATTENTION TO HER SHE OPENS THE DOOR AND SAYS WHY ARE YOU YELLING AND WHAT DO YOU WANT BJ SAYS CAN WE PLEASE TALK KENEKA SAYS YEAH OK COME IN BJ SITS ON THE COUCH AND BEGINS TO APOLOGIZE FOR EVERYTHING HE DID TO HER AND HE ASKS HER FOR ANOTHER CHANCE KENEKA AGREED BUT SOON SHE WOULD REGRET SHE DID SO BJ MOVES IN WITH KENEKA AND THEY GOT BACK TOGETHER THINGS SEEMED LIKE THEY WAS GOING GOOD FOR THE MOMENT

TWO MONTHS PAST BJ WAS STILL STAYING WITH KENEKA KENEKA WAS OUT WORKING AND SHE DESIDED TO PARK THE TRUCK EARLY SHE WAS TIRED SO THE NEXT DAY KENEKA GETS A CALL FROM HER JOB ASKING HER WHY SHE PARKED THE TRUCK EARLY AND KENEKA TOLD THEM SHE WAS FALLING A SLEEP BEHIND THE WHEEL SO SHE PARKED IT THE BOSS REPLIED WELL WE GOTTA LET YOU GO BECAUSE YOU WHERE SUPPOSE TO KEEP THE TRUCK MOVING TILL 4PM KENEKA SAID WHAT !!!! IT WAS ONLY 30 MINUTES EARLY ARE YOU SERIOUS HER BOSS SAID YES I AM AND ILL BE SENDING ANOTHER DRIVER TO GET THE KEYS

FROM YOU NOW KENEKA REPLIED YEAH OK WHAT EVER AND HUNG UP THE PHONE 30 MINTUES LATER THE DRIVER ARRIVES AND GETS THE KEYS FROM KENEKA AND TAKES OFF IN THE TRUCK KENEKA GOT REAL DEPRESSED AGAIN SO THE NEXT MORNING KENEKA WENT JOB SEARCHING KENEKA SEEN ON CRAIGSLIST THAT SUPPER SHUTTLE WAS HIRING SO KENEKA TOOK A TRIP TO THE AIRPORT TO PUT IN A APPLICATION AND THEY TOLD HER THANKS FOR APPLYING AFTER WE REVIEW YOUR APPLICATION WE WILL MAKE A DECISION AND GIVE YOU A CALL IF YOUR APPLICATION MEETS THE REQUIREMENTS KENEKA

REPLIES OK GREAT THANKS AND HEADS BACK TO THE BUS STOP AT THE AIRPORT WHILE WAITING ON THE BUS KENEKA RUNS ACROSS HER COUSIN T SHE WAS SO HAPPY TO SEE HER T SPEAKS HEY WHAT YOU DOING OUT HERE KENEKA REPLIES I JUST PUT A APPLICATION IN AT SUPER SHUTTLE T REPLIES OH OK I HOPE YOU GET THE JOB I WORK OUT HERE TO KENEKA REPLIES OH REALLY T REPLIES YES I DO KENEKA REPLIES OH OK AND T ASK KENEKA HAVE YOU FOUND YOUR BROTHER DEE YET KENEKA REPLIES NO I HAVE BEEN WONDERING WHERE HE IS FOR YEARS BUT AINT HAD NO LUCK FINDING HIM T REPLIES I GOT HIS

NUMBER KENKEA SCREAMS WHAT!!!!!
CAN I HAVE IT PLEASE T GOES IN HER
PURSE AND GETS SOME PEN AND PAPER
AND WRITES IT DOWN FOR HER KENEKA
HUGS T AND SAYS THANK YOU SO MUCH I
HAVE BEEN WANTING MY BROTHER IN
MY LIFE FOR MANY YEARS BUT DIDN'T
KNOW WHERE HE WAS MY MOM TOLD
ME ABOUT HIM WHEN I WAS YOUNGER  T
RELPIES YOUR SO WELCOME MAKE SURE
YOU CALL HIM KENEKA REPLIES OH I
WILL T HEADS INTO THE AIRPORT TO GO
TO WORK AND TELLS KENEKA  ILL SEE
YOU LATER KENEKA REPLIES OK ABOUT
5 MINUTES LATER THE BUS PULLS UP
KENEKA JUMPS ON KENEKA WAS FILLED

WITH JOY BUT SHE ALSO GOT NERVOUS
SHE DIDN'T KNOW WHAT TO SAY TO DEE
WHEN SHE CALLED HIM KENEKA SAT
THERE WITH THE PHONE IN HER HAND
JUST LOOKING AT THE NUMBER AND
STILL COULDN'T BELIEVE SHE FOUND
ONE OF HER BROTHERS ABOUT 5
MINTUES LATER SHE CALLED AND A MAN
ANSWERED THE PHONE KENEKA SAID
CAN I SPEAK TO DEE PLEASE THE MAN
SAID SURE HOLD ON KENEKA WAS
GETTING VERY NERVOUS WHILE SHE
WAITED FOR HIM TO COME TO THE
PHONE ALL OF A SUDDEN KENEKA
HEARED HIM SAY HELLO SHE FROZE FOR
A SECOND DEE SAID HELLO AGAIN

KENEKA REPLIED HI THIS IS YOUR
SISTER KENEKA T GAVE ME YOUR
NUMBER DEE SCREAMED OMG SIS…
KENEKA REPLIED YEAH ITS ME DEE SAID
HOW YOU BEEN DOING I AM GLAD TO
HEAR FROM YOU IVE BEEN LOOKING FOR
YOU KENEKA SAID OK I AM GOOD THEN
DEE RELPIED I AM AT WORK RIGHT NOW
BUT GIVE ME YOUR NUMBER AND ILL
CALL YOU LATER WHEN I GET OFF WORK
KENEKA SAID OK AND GAVE DEE HER
NUMBER AND DEE SAID OK SIS ILL CALL
YOU LATER I LOVE YOU AND KENEKA
REPLIED I LOVE YOU TO AND HUG UP
THE PHONE KENEKA WAS SO SHOCKED
THAT SHE HAD JUST TALKED TO HER

BROTHER KENEKA HEADS BACK HOME WHEN KENEKA GETS HOME HER HOUSE IS A MESS KENEKA GETS MAD AND YELLS AT BJ WHY IS MY HOUSE DIRTY IT WASNT DIRTY WHEN I LEFT BJ RESPONDS I AM SORRY ILL CLEAN IT UP KENEKA REPLIES YEAH YOU BETTER I AINT CLEANING UP AFTER NO GROWN MAN BJ JUST LOOK AT HER AND SAYS YEAH OK AND BJ BEGINS TO CLEAN IT UP KENEKA GOES IN HER ROOM TO RELAX AND WATCH TV AND LAY DOWN ABOUT 3 HOURS LATER KENEKA GETS A CALL FROM A OUT OF TOWN NUMBER AND SHE ANSWERS HELLO... HEY SIS ITS ME KENEKA REPLIES HEY IS THIS YOUR

CELLPHONE NUMBER DEE REPLIES YES SIS KENEKA REPLIES OK ILL LOCK IT IN DEE REPLIES OK AND BEGINS TALKING TO KENEKA ABOUT EVERYTHING AS KENEKA IS ON THE PHONE BJ WALKS IN THE ROOM WITH HER AND BJ HERES A MAN TALKING ON THE PHONE WITH KENEKA THEN BJ BEGINS TO YELL AT KENEKA AS SAYS WHO IS THAT ON THE PHONE KENEKA JUST LOOKS AT HIM WITH A EVIL LOOK ON HER FACE AND DEE ASK WHO IS THAT TALKING TO YOU LIKE THAT PUT THAT MAN ON THE PHONE I DONT KNOW WHO HE THINK HE TALKING TO PUT HIM ON THE DAMN PHONE NOW KENEKA GIVES BJ THE

PHONE BJ SAYS WHO THE HELL IS THIS THEN AFTER DEE SPEAKS HE APOLOGIZES TO DEE AND GIVES KENEKA THE PHONE BACK KENEKA SAYS TO BJ YOU NEED TO STOP THE INSECURE BULL CRAP FOR REAL AND KENEKA CONTINUES TO TALK TO DEE , DEE SAYS TO KENEKA I DONT WANNA HAVE TO MESS THAT MAN UP SIS CAUSE I WILL HE BETTER CLAIM THAT DOWN KENEKA SAYS I KNOW ... BJ JUST LOOKS AT KENEKA CAUSE HE KNOW HER BROTHER IS SNAPPING AND TALKING ABOUT HIM DEE WAS HEATED DEE TALKS TO KENEKA FOR ABOUT 5 MORE MINUTES AND SAYS OK SIS ILL TALK TO YOU

LATER I GOTTA GO I LOVE YOU KENEKA REPLIES I LOVE YOU TO AND HANGS UP AFTER KENEKA HANGS UP THE PHONE SHE JUMPS OUT THE BED AND GOES IN THE LIVING ROOM AND SAYS TO BJ WHO THE HELL DO YOU THINK YOU ARE COMING AT ME ASKING ME WHO I AM TALKING TO YOU ARE A VERY INSECURE MAN FOR NO REASON AT ALL ILL GIVE YOU A REASON TO BE ACCUSING ME KEEP PLAYING WITH ME AND ILL SHOW YOU BETTER THAN I CAN TELL YOU I AINT NO CHEATER YOU UP IN MY HOUSE AND YOU WILL RESPECT ME IN MY HOUSE !!!!! BJ JUST LOOKS AT HER AND SAYS NOTHING KENEKA TURNS AROUND

AND GOES BACK TO HER ROOM  AND
GOES TO SLEEP FOR THE NIGHT THE
NEXT MORNING KENEKA WAKES UP TO
HER PHONE RINGING KENEKA PICKS IT
UP AND SAYS HELLO... THEY REPLIES HI
IS KENEKA AVAILABLE KENEKA REPLIES
SPEAKING ... HE REPLIES HI KENEKA
THIS IS MACK I WAS CALLING YOU
BECAUSE I RECEIVED YOUR
APPLICATION AND I WAS WONDERING IF
YOU COULD COME IN FOR A INTERVIEW
TODAY AT 1PM KENEKA REPLIES YES... I
CAN MACK REPLIES OK GREAT SEE YOU
AT 1PM KENEKA REPLIES OK THANKS
AND HANGS UP KENEKA GETS OUT OF
BED AND GETS DRESSED BJ STARTS

AGAIN WHERE YOU GOING ALL DRESSED UP YOU GOING TO SEE A MAN KENEKA REPLIES DID YOU REALLY JUST ASK ME THAT GET OUT MY FACE BJ KENEKA GRABS HER PURSE AND GOES OUT THE DOOR TO HEAD TO HER INTERVIEW KENEKA ARRIVES 30 MINUTES EARLY AFTER THE INTERVIEW MACK SAYS TO KENEKA CAN YOU START TOMORROW AT 11AM KENEKA REPLIES YES I CAN MACK REPLIES OK GREAT SEE YOU TOMORROW AT 11AM AND SHAKES KENEKA HAND KENEKA REPLIES OK THANKS SEE YOU IN THE MORNING KENEKA HEADS BACK HOME WHEN KENEKA ARRIVES HOME BJ LOOKS AT HER WITH A EVIL LOOK ON

HIS FACE KENEKA SAYS YOU GOT A PROBLEM BJ SAYS YEAH I KNOW YOU JUST WENT TO SEE SOME DUDE KENEKA REPLIES YEAH I SURE DID MY BOSS START MY JOB IN THE MORNING SO WHILE YOU SITTING YOUR FAT BEHING UP IN MY HOUSE STILL TRYING TO SAY I AM MESSING AROUND YOU NEED TO GET OFF YOUR FAT BEHIND AND CLEAN UP MY HOUSE I LEAVE MY HOUSE CLEAN AND COME BACK AND ITS MESSED UP AND YOU KNOW WHAT ELSE YOU CAN DO GO GET A JOB AND HELP PAY SOME OF THESE BILLS !!!!! KENEKA TURNS AND WALKS INTO HER ROOM KENEKA BEGINS HER JOB THE NEXT MORNING KENEKA

WAS DOING GOOD A MONTH HAD PAST AND SHE WAS STILL WORKING AT SUPER SHUTTLE THEN ALL OF A SUDDEN KENEKA GETS A CALL FROM BJ WHILE SHES DRIVING ON THE HIGH WAY SHE HIT THE END BUTTON CAUSE SHE HAD CUSTOMERS IN HER VAN AT THE MOMENT SO AFTER KENEKA DROPPED OF HER CUSTOMERS AT THE AIRPORT SHE STARTS DRIVING BACK TO THE WAITING AREA TO WAIT FOR HER NEXT CALL TO RETURN TO THE AIRPORT TO PICK UP MORE CUSTOMERS AS SHE DRIVING KENEKA CHECKS HER MESSAGES SHE HAD 1 MESSAGE FROM BJ AS SHE IS TRYING TO LISTEN TO IT BJ

CALLS AGAIN KENEKA ANSWERS IT
HELLO… BJ REPLIES YEAH I SEE YOU
WITH THAT MAN I AM SITTING HERE
LOOKING AT YOU RIGHT NOW WHILE
YOU SITING THERE  KENEKA REPLIES
WHAT  !!! KENEKA CUSSES FIRST OFF ALL
YOU LIEING IF YOU WAS LOOKING AT ME
RIGHT NOW YOU WOULD KNOW AINT NO
BODY IN MY CAR AND I AM ON THE HIGH
WAY SO HOW ARE YOU JUST SITTING
THERE WATCHING ME GET OFF MY LINE
WITH THAT BS KENEKA HANGS UP BJ
CALLS RIGHT BACK KENEKA TURNS HER
PHONE OFF  KENEKA GOES BACK TO
WORKING HER SHIFT KENEKA WAS
GETTING TIRED OF HIM SAYING SHE WAS

DOING SOMETHING WHEN SHE WASN'T DOING NOTHING ... KENEKA HEADED HOME 2 HOURS LATER WHEN SHE GETS HOME SHE PARKS HER WORK VAN AND GOES IN THE HOUSE BJ WAS SITTING THERE PLAYING ON THE GAME KENEKA LOOKS AT HIM EVIL AFTER LOOKING AT HER HOUSE KENEKA SAYS WHY IS MY HOUSE DIRTY AND WHY YOU JUST SITTING HERE ON THE GAME ALL DAY YOU NEED TO GO OUT AND FIND A JOB INSTEAD OF SITTING ON YOUR BUTT ALL DAY BOTHERING ME WHILE I AM AT WORK ABOUT NOTHING BJ REPLIES I AINT GOT NO BUS FARE KENEKA REPLIES YOU ARE A SORRY EXCUSE FOR A MAN

YOU BEEN STAYING HERE RENT FREE FOR MONTHS DOING NOTHING AND DIRTYING UP MY HOUSE AND NOT CLEANING UP BJ CUSSES AT HER KENEKA REPLIES WHATS WRONG THE TRUTH HURTS HUH KENEKA PULLS OUT 20.00 AND PUTS IT ON THE TABLE AND SAYS GO FIND A JOB NOW YOU AINT GOT NO EXCUSE BJ JUST LOOKS AT HER AND SAYS YEAH OK KENEKA GOES TO HER ROOM AND BJ KEPT PLAYING THE GAME FOR THE NEXT COUPLE WEEKS BJ WENT JOB SEARING WHILE KENEKA WAS AT WORK AND AFTER 2 WEEKS WHEN KENEKA GOT HOME BJ SAYS GUESS WHAT I GOT A INTERVIEW IN THE

MORNING AT THE RAILROAD KENEKA
REPLIED GOOD ABOUT TIME THE NEXT
MORNING BJ WENT TO HIS INTERVIEW
AND GOT THE JOB KENEKA WAS VERY
HAPPY AT THE TIME KENEKA HAD 2 CARS
SHE HAD A RED VAN AND A BLACK
BLAZER KENEKA LET BJ TAKE THE
BLACK BLAZER BACK AND FORTH TO
WORK EVEN THOUGH SHE WAS TRYING
TO SELL IT CAUSE SHE HAD JUST GOT
THE VAN SO BJ TOOK HER BLACK TRUCK
BACK AND FORTH TO WORK EVERYDAY
ABOUT A MONTH LATER BJ WAS STILL
DOING GOOD AND STILL HAD HIS JOB
AND KENEKA STILL HAD HERS THE NEXT
WEEK KENEKA CAME HOME JUST

GETTING OFF OF WORK IT WAS ABOUT 10PM KENEKA WALKS IN THE HOUSE AND SHE SEES 5 MEN SITTING IN HER LIVING ROOM KENEKA YELLS BJ WHY ARE THERE MEN IN MY HOUSE AND YOU AINT ASK ME FIRST HOW YOU JUST GOING TO BRING PEOPLE IN MY HOUSE I DONT KNOW ONE OF BJS BOY SAYS HEY BABY GIRL WE JUST KICKING IT AIN'T NOTHING TO GET MAD ABOUT KENEKA LOOKS AT HIM AND SAYS FIRST OF ALL I WASN'T TALKING TO YOU AND I AIN'T YOUR BABY GIRL SO MIND YOUR BUSINESS THE MAN CUSSES AND SAYS OK BJ TELLS KENEKA TO COME IN THE ROOM FOR A MINUTE THEN BJ ASK WHY

YOU TRIPING THESE ARE MY BOYS FROM WORK KENEKA REPLIES WHAT YOU MEAN WHY AM I TRIPPING I CANT WALK AROUND MY HOUSE LIKE I WANT TO AND RELAX CAUSE YOU GOT MEN IN MY LIVING ROOM AND ITS LATE BJ JUST LOOKS AT HER AND WALKS BACK OUT TO THE LIVING ROOM AND TELLS HIS BOYS THEY HAD TO RAP IT UP AND HIS BOYS LEAVE AND KENEKA BEGINS TO RELAX AND GET READY TO GO TO BED SO THEY BOTH KEEP WORKING THEN THE FOLLOWING WEEK KENEKA GETS OFF AND COMES HOME THINKING SHES ABOUT TO RELAX SHE WALKS IN THE HOUSE TO SEE HIS BOYS ALL IN HER

LIVING ROOM KENEKA LOOKS AT BJ EVIL AND KEEPS WALKING TO HER ROOM KENEKA WAS ABOUT TO SHOW HIM SINCE HE WASNT RESPECTING WHAT SHE ASKED HIM SO KENEKA PUTS HER SEXY NIGHY ON THAT WAS SUPPER SHORT AND YOU COULD SEE HER BEHIND IT WAS VERY SHORT AND HER CHEST WAS SITTING UP HIGH SO AFTER PUTTING IT ON KENEKA WALKS OUT TO THE LIVING ROOM AND SAYS HOW YOU DOING FELLAS ALL OF THERE EYES GOT BUCK BJ TURNS AROUND AND CUSSES AND TRYS TO COVER HER UP AND LOOKS AT HIS BOYS THEY WHERE LOOKING HARD HE SAYS TO THE WHAT YALL

LOOKING AT GET OUT MY HOUSE NOW!!!! HIS BOYS GET UP AND LEAVE STILL LOOKING AT KENEKA ONCE THEY ALL GOT OUT BJ SAYS WHAT THE HELL ARE YOU DOING KENEKA REPLIES I TOLD YOU NOT TO HAVE THEM IN MY HOUSE LATE AND YOU KEPT DIS RESPECTING ME ANYWAY SO I DECIDED TO WALK AROUND MY HOUSE HOW I WANT TO WITH THEM HERE I AIN'T PLAYING WITH YOU SO NOW YOU KNOW …. KENEKA TURNS AND GOES BACK TO HER ROOM BJ JUST KEPT STANDING THERE HE COULDN'T BELIEVE SHE JUST DID THAT…. SO AFTER THAT BJ STOPPED DOING IT SO FOR THE NEXT COUPLE

MONTHS SHE WAS ABLE TO COME HOME AND RELAX THE NEXT WEEK KENEKA HAD THE DAY OFF SO SHE RAN OUT TO RUN SOME ARRON'S AND GRAB SOME MORE FOOD FOR THE HOUSE THEN GOES BACK HOME AND STARTED COOKING AND CLEANING WHILE SHES COOKING SOME BOILED CHICKEN AND POTATOES SHE GETS A CALL FROM BJ SHE ANSWERS IT HELLO... BJ REPLIES CAN I BRING THE BOYS OVER FOR A LITTLE BIT KENEKA REPLIES OK BJ SAYS OK BE THERE SOON AND HANGS UP ABOUT 30 MINUTES LATER  BJ GETS THERE WITH HIS BOYS WHEN THEY COME IN THEY SEE KENEKA IN THE KICTHEN COOKING AND THEY

SAY TO KENEKA HI MISS LADY HOW YOU DOING TODAY KENEKA REPLIES I AM FINE THEN HIS BOYS SIT DOWN KENEKA KEEPS WALKING BACK AND FORTH CHECKING THE FOOD WHILE SHE WAS IN HER ROOM WATCHING TV THEN BJ COMES IN THE ROOM AND SAYS I THINK YOU GOT TO MUCH WATER IN THAT POT KENEKA REPLIES NO I DONT I KNOW HOW TO COOK THEN BJ GOES BACK IN THE LIVING ROOM WITH HIS BOYS THEN KENEKA WALKS OUT TO CHECK THE FOOD AGAIN AND BJ COMES IN THE KITCHEN AND SAYS SO WHOS THAT DUDE THAT WAS HERE I SAW HIM AS I WAS PULLING UP COMING OUT KENEKA

REPLIES WHAT !!!! HE WAS PROBLY NEXT DOOR HE AINT COME OUT OF MY HOUSE BJ SAYS NO HE DIDNT KENEKA SAYS YOU KNOW WHAT GO BACK IN THERE WITH YOUR BOYS AND LEAVE ME ALONE WITH THAT BS BJ REPLIES NO WHO WAS THAT DUDE KENEKA GETS BEYOND PISSED AND CUSSES AT HIM AND SAYS GET OUT MY FACE BJ REPLIES NO WHAT YOU GOING TO DO ABOUT IT MAKE ME GET OUT YOUR FACE KENEKA PICKS UP THE BOILING POT OF CHICKEN AND THROWS IT ON HIM SO FAST HE DIDN'T SEE IT COMING BJ FALLS TO THE FLOOR SCREAMING AND CUSSING BJS BOYS EYES GOT BUCK THEY COULDNT BELIEVE SHE

THREW A POT OF CHICKEN ON HIM THEY ALL GOT UP AND SAID ALRIGHT BJ WE WILL CATCH YOU LATER MAN AND RAN OUT THE DOOR KENEKA YELLED YEAH GET OUT MY HOUSE ... THEY SCATTERED LIKE ROACHES THEN KENEKA SAID SINCE YOU WANNA KEEP STARTING STUFF WITH ME YOU COOK YOUR OWN FOOD I AM GOING OUT TO EAT BYE BJ WAS IN SHOCK HE COULDN'T BELIEVE SHE THREW A POT OF HOT CHICKEN ON HIM HE SAT THERE LOOKING FOR ABOUT 2 MINUTES THEN AS KENEKA WENT OUT THE DOOR HE TRIED TO GET UP AND CHASE HER BUT HE FELL BACK ON THE FLOOR AGAIN BECAUSE THE FLOOR WAS

SLIPPERY FROM ALL THE WATER ON THE FLOOR KENEKA JUMPED IN HER VAN AND WENT TO DENNYS TO EAT DINNER AND CLAIM DOWN KENEKA SAID TO HER SELF DID I REALLY JUST DO THAT I AIN'T NEVER DID THAT TO NO ONE IN MY LIFE KENEKA STARTED TO SEE THAT HE WAS TURNING  HER INTO A VERY ANGRY PERSON SHE HAD KNOCKED HIM OUT TWICE AND NOW SHE THREW A POT OF HOT CHICKEN ON HIM KENEKA BEGIN TO THINK WHATS WRONG WITH ME THIS AIN'T EVEN ME AT ALL BUT THE FACT IS BJ KEPT S PUSHING KENEKA AND ACCUSING HER OF SOMETHING SHE AIN'T DOING AND HE KEEPS COMING OUT THE

WOOD WORK WITH RANDOM STUFF HE HAS SOME REAL INSURANCE ISSUES  AND WAS VERY CONTROLLING AT TIMES WELL HE TRY ED TO BE BUT KENEKA WASN'T GOING FOR IT AFTER EATING KENEKA HEADED BACK TO THE HOUSE WHEN SHE WALKED IN BJ WAS SITTING THERE EATING THAT CHICKEN SHE THREW ALL OVER THE FLOOR AND BJ JUST LOOKED AT HER AND DIDN'T SAY NOTHING KENEKA WENT TO HER ROOM AND WENT TO BED FOR THE NIGHT AND THEY BOTH CONTINUED WORKING EVERYDAY      ANOTHER 2 MONTHS PAST BJ STILL KEEP ACCUSING HER WHEN SHE WASNT DOING NOTHING BUT

WORKING AND COMING HOME TO HIM EVERYDAY KENEKA GOT TO A POINT THAT SHE DIDNT EVEN WANNA BE IN HERE OWN HOUSE WITH HIM BECAUSE HE GOT TO A POINT HE WAS STARTING STUFF WITH HER EVERYDAY , EVERYDAY IT WAS A ARGUMENT FOR NO REASON AT ALL SO KENEKA CHANGED HER ROUTINE INSTEAD OF STAYING IN THE HOUSE AFTER WORK WAS OVER KENEKA STARTED GOING OUT EVERY NIGHT WITH HER GIRL  LA THEY WENT TO THE MOOSE EVERY NIGHT AND WAS SHOOTING POOL AND DRINKING KENEKA WOULD DRINK 3-4 LONG ISLAND A NIGHT AND SHOOT POOL WITH LA KENEKA WAS

HAVING A BALL WITH LA KENEKA DID THIS FOR THE NEXT 2-3 MONTHS STRAIGHT IT WAS HER WAY OF GETTING AWAY FROM BJ AND AVOIDING ARGUMENTS EVERY NIGHT NOW WHEN KENEKA CAME IN SHE WAS DRUNK AND WENT STRAIGHT TO BED SO BJ DIDN'T BOTHER HER WHILE SHE WAS DRUNK CAUSE SHE WAS OUT OF IT HE WOULD JUST LOOK AT HER EVERY NIGHT WHEN SHE CAME IN LIKE THAT BUT ONE NIGHT HE SAID TO HER WHY ARE YOU DOING THIS EVERY NIGHT THAT AIN'T YOU!!!! KENEKA STUCK UP HER MIDDLE FINGER AT HIM AND TOOK HER DRUNK BUTT TO BED AFTER THE 3RD MONTH STRAIGHT

OF GOING OUT KENEKA COULDN'T KEEP UP WITH IT SHE GOT SO BAD SHE KEPT BEING LATE FOR WORK AND ENDED UP LOOSING HER JOB WITH SUPER SHUTTLE SO NOW KENEKA WAS JOB LESS AGAIN BECUASE OF THE STRESS SHE WAS DEALING WITH AND THE CHOICES SHE MADE TO GET AWAY FROM BJ SO ANOTHER 2 WEEKS PAST AND BJ ENDED UP LOSING HIS JOB BECAUSE HE WENT OFF ON THE BOSS AT WORK SO NOW THEY WHERE BOTH JOB LESS 6 MONTHS LATER BJ AND KENEKA STILL DIDNT HAVE WORK THEN KENEKAS LANDLORD CAME BY AND ASKED KENEKA IF SHE HAD FOUND A JOB YET KENEKA REPLIED

NO NOT YET THEN BEN SAID WELL I
HAVE GAVE YOU SIX MONTHS TO FIND
SOMETHING SO YOU HAVE BEEN HERE
SIX MONTHS WITH OUT PAYING RENT I
CANT WAIT ANYMORE I AM GOING TO
HAVE TO GO FILE FOR EVICTION I CANT
WAIT ANY LONGER KENEKA REPLIED
WHAT !!!! OK I UNDERSTAND YOU HAVE
BEEN VERY PATIENT WITH ME AND WAS
NICE ENOUGH TO LET ME STAY THIS
LONG SO ILL WORK ON GETTING SOME
WHERE ELSE TO GO BEN REPLIES I AM
SORRY KENEKA AND WALKS AWAY....
KENEKA CLOSES THE DOOR AND
SCREAMS SHE CUSSES ... THEN KENEKA
JUMPS ON THE PHONE WITH DIFFERENT

FAMILY MEMBERS TO SEE IF ONE OF THEM CAN HELP HER KENEKA GOT LUCKY HER COUSIN WILL SAID SHE COULD MOVE IN WITH HE HE STAYED RIGHT AROUND THE CONNER FROM HER SO SHE STARTED PACKING HER STUFF THE NEXT WEEK AND BJ HAD TO RETURN TO THE SHELTER CAUSE HE COULDN'T GO TO HER COUSINS HOUSE WITH HER KENEKA WAS GLAD ABOUT THAT KENEKA MOVED IN WITH HER COUSIN A WEEK LATER AFTER THE FIRST MONTH OF STAYING THERE HER COUSIN ENDED UP IN JAIL SO KENEKA WAS TRYING TO FIGURE OUT HOW SHE COULD CONTACT THE LANDLORD TO PAY THE RENT SO

KENEKA CALLED HER COUSINS BROTHER AND ASKED HIM WHO HIS BROTHERS LANDLORD WAS HE REPLIED HE AIN'T GOT NO LANDLORD HE IS STAYING IN A ABANDONED HOUSE KENEKA REPINED WHAT!!! HIS BROTHER REPLIED YEAH … AND SAID PLEASE DON'T TELL ME YOU ARE STAYING WITH HIM KENEKA REPLIED YEAH I AM… HE REPLIED OH NO HONEY YOU BETTER FIND ANOTHER PLACE SOON BEFORE THEY FIND OUT YOUR IN THERE KENEKA REPLIED SHOOT OK THANKS FOR LETTING ME KNOW HE REPLIES NO PROBLEM TALK TO YOU LATER KENEKA SAID OK BYE AND HUNG UP KENEKA DECIDED TO STAY THERE

LONGER CAUSE THE LIGHTS AND EVERYTHING WAS STILL ON AND SHE NEEDED MORE TIME ABOUT 2 WEEKS LATER SHE GOT A CALL FROM WALMART SHE HAD APPLY ED WITH THEM ABOUT A MONTH AGO THEY ASKED HER TO GO IN FOR A INTERVIEW SO SHE DID AND SHE GOT THE JOB AND STARTED WORKING SHORTY AFTER THE INTERVIEW AFTER WORKING FOR ABOUT 3 WEEKS SHE FOUND A PLACE IT WAS THREW HER MOMS LANDLORD HE HAD A ROOM FOR RENT IN THE BASEMENT OF THE DUPLEX HER MOM STAYED IN SO KENEKA TOOK IT AND MOVED IN A COUPLE DAYS LATER SHE GOT ALL UNPACED AND SETTLED IN

SHE WAS HAPPY SHE GOT SOMETHING
QUICK SO SHE COULD GET OUT OF THE
ABANDONED HOUSE BJ CALLED KENEKA
LATER THAT DAY TO SEE WHERE SHE
WAS THEN HE HARED HER MOM IN THE
BACKGROUND THEN BJ SAID OH YOU
BACK AT YOUR MOMS HUH OK ILL BE
THERE SOON KENEKA HUNG UP THE
PHONE AND SAID DANG IT …. SEE
COULDN'T TRY TO COVER IT UP CAUSE
HER RED VAN WAS PARKED OUT SIDE SO
HE WOULD KNOW SHE WAS THERE
ANYWAY WHEN BJ GOT THERE KENEKA
LET HIM IN HIS MOMS HE DIDNT KNOW
SHE WAS IN THE ROOM IN THE
BASEMENT BUT SHE WANTED TO KEEP IT

LIKE THAT FOR AS LONG AS SHE COULD WHEN BJ GOT UP STAIRS HE SAID HI MS.HARRIS HOW YOU DOING SHE RESPONDED I AM GOOD THAT S GOOD BJ REPLIED THEN BJ AND KENEKAS MOM KEPT TALKING FOR ALONG TIME ABOUT ALOT OF THINGS THEN OUT OF NO WHERE KENEKA BEING TOUCHED AS A KID CAME OUT OF BJS MOUTH KENEKA BEGIN TO FEEL UNCOMFORTABLE BECAUSE HE WAS TALKING ABOUT IT TO HER MOM WITH HER SITTING THERE KENEKAS MOM GOT OFFENDED REAL QUICK THEN BJ GOT TO TALKING ABOUT SOMETHINGS KENEKA WAS TALKING TO HIM ABOUT BJ BEGIN TO SAY TO

KENEKAS MOM ALL THESE YEARS SHE HAS BEEN HURTING BECAUSE YOU DIDN'T BELIEVE HER WHEN SHE WAS A CHILD AND YOU KEPT TALKING TO HIM EVEN AFTER HE WAS LOCKED UP KENEKAS MOM REPLIED THAT WAS YEARS AGO SHE NEED TO GET OVER THAT BJ REPLIED NO !!!! SHE HASN'T GOTTEN OVER IT BECAUSE IT AIN'T EASY TO GET OVER AND YOU NEVER APOLOGIZED TO HER SO ALL THESE YEARS SHE BEEN HOLDING ON TO THE FACT THAT YOU NEVER EVEN SAID YOU WHERE SORRY AND SHE FEELS LIKE YOU DON'T LOVE HER BECAUSE YOU NEVER APOLOGIZE TO HER BY THIS TIME

KENEKA WAS IN TEARS AS BJ EXPLAIN TO
HER MOM HOW SHE FELT THEN
KENEKAS MOM STARTED CRYING AND
HUGGED KENEKA AND APOLOGIZED TO
HER AND TOLD KENEKA I DO LOVE YOU
YOU KNOW THAT RIGHT KENEKA
REPLIED NOW I DO BUT I DINT THINK
YOU DID KENEKA MOMS HOLDS HER TILL
SHE CLAMS DOWN THEN BJ SAID SEE ALL
THESE YEARS AND IT TOOK ME TO SAY
SOMETHING FOR HER TO HEAR YOU SAY
THAT TO HER NOW I AM GLAD THAT WAS
FINALLY SAID BJ GOT OFF THE SUBJECT
AND STARTED TALKING ABOUT
SOMETHING ELSE THEN A COUPLE
HOURS LATER BJ HEADED BACK TO THE

SHELTER FOR THE NIGHT  THE NEXT WEEK THE HEALING POSSES STARTED FOR KENEKA BEING HER MOM FINALLY SAID SORRY KENEKA WASN'T SURE WHY SHE FELT LIKE THAT BUT SHE DID ABOUT 2 WEEKS AFTER THAT KENEKA WROTE A LETTER TO AJ THE ONE WHO WAS TOUCHING HER AS A KID AND SHE STOPPED BY HIS MOMS CAUSE THAT'S WHERE HE LIVED IN HIS MOMS HOUSE SO SHE DROPPED THE LETTER IN THE BOX AND DROPPED IT OFF  SHE TOLD HIM SHE WANTED TO KNOW WHY HE DID WHAT HE DID TO HER AND SHE WANTED TO SEE HIM IN PERSON A COUPLE DAYS LATER HE CALLS KENEKA AND TELLS HER TO

STOP BY SO KENEKA DOES WHEN SHE GETS THERE SHE WAS GREETED BY HIS MOTHER KENEKA LOVED AJS MOM SHE TOLD KENEKA TO COME ON IN SO KENEKA WALK IN AND SAT ON THE COUCH HIS MOM BEGINS TO TALK SHE SAYS TO KENEKA I AM SO SORRY FOR WHAT MY SON DID TO YOU I WENT OFF ON HIM ONCE I FOUND OUT WHAT HE DID AND I AM SO SORRY KENEKA HIS MOM HUGS HER CAUSE KENEKA STARTS CRYING AFTER KENEKA CLAIMS DOWN AJS MOM SAYS ASK HIM WHAT YOU WANNA ASK HIM KENEKA BEGINS TO TALK AND SAYS WHY DID YOU DO THAT TO ME .... AJ REPLIES I DON'T HAVE NO

EXPLANATION FOR WHY I DID BUT REGARDLESS OF WHY I DID IT IT WAS WRONG AND I AM VERY SORRY I HURT YOU LIKE THAT KENEKA REPLIED I FORGIVE YOU THEN AJS MOM REPLIED AGAIN I AM SO SORRY FOR WHAT MY SON DID TO YOU AND SHE HUGGED KENEKA AGAIN THEN KENEKA SAID OK I GOTTA GET GOING I JUST NEEDED TO FACE HIM AND GET A ANSWER HIS MOM REPLIED I UNDERSTAND KENEKA REPLIED OK AND THEN KENEKA LEFT AFTER THAT KENEKA FELT LIKE SOME WEIGHT LIFTED OFF HER SHOULDERS SHE WASN'T SURE WHY BUT SHE BEGIN TO THINK THAT WAS PART OF WHAT SHE

NEEDED TO FINALLY START HEALING SHE NEEDED TO FORGIVE HIM NOT FOR HIM BUT FOR HER KENEKA THEN GOT BACK IN HER CAR AND HEADED BACK HOME TO GET READY FOR WORK AT WALMART FROM 4 TO CLOSE WHEN KENEKA GOT OFF LATER THAT NIGHT SHE GOT A CALL FROM BJ SHE ANSWERED BJ SAID WHERE YOU AT AND WHAT YOU DOING YOU WITH A DUDE RIGHT NOW KENEKA SAID ARE YOU SERIOUS RIGHT NOW YOU KNOW WHAT I AM DONE WITH YOU AND YOUR INSECURITIES LEAVE ME ALONE AND KENEKA HUNG UP AND  THREE WEEKS LATER KENEKA HADN'T  HEARD FROM BJ

SHE WAS SHOCKED AND HAPPY ABOUT 6 MONTHS PAST KENEKA WAS TILL WORKING AT WALMART AND SHE DIDNT HEAR ANYTHING ELSE FROM BJ AFTER SHE TOLD HIM TO LEAVE HER ALONE KENEKA HAD A DAY OFF SHE DECIDED TO JUST RELAX IN THE HOUSE ABOUT A HOUR LATER KENEKA WANTED SOMETHING SWEET SO SHE GOT UP AND WALKED AROUND THE CORNER TO THE GAS STATION WHEN SHE GOT OVER THERE SHE SEEN BLACK WALKING SHE YELLED HEY BLACK HE TRUNED AND LOOKED AND SEEN IT WAS KENEKA SO HE STARTED WALKING TOWARDS HER BLACK BEGINS TALKING THEY TALK FOR

A FEW MINUTES THEN KENEKA RUNS IN THE STORE TO GET HER SNACKS AND COMES BACK OUT HER AND BLACK WALK BACK AROUND THE CORNER TO HER HOUSE BLACK STAYS FOR ABOUIT A HOUR THEN BLACK LEAVES AND TELLS HER ILL CALL YOU LATER KENEKA REPLIES OK AND BLACK LEAVES KENEKA GOT VERY EXCITED SHE HAD SO MUCH LOVE FOR HIM SHE DIDN'T EVEN UNDERSTAND IT HER SELF BUT SHE KNOW IT WAS REAL CAUSE ALL THE TIME HE WAS GONE SHE WOULD STILL THINK ABOUT HIM AND WAS USING HIS BIRTH YEAR FOR HER CODE TO HE PHONE KENEKA LAYED IN BED

WATCHING MOVIES THINKING ABOUT BLACK THE REST OF THE DAY HE TEXTED HER LATER THAT NIGHT AND TALKED TO HER MORE THEN THE NEXT DAY AFTER KENEKA WAS DONE WITH HER SHIFT SHE GOT A EXTRA KEY MADE CAUSE SHE WANTED BLACK TO HAVE A KEY TO GET IN WHEN EVER HE WANTED TO SO SHE GOT A KEY MADE THEN HURRIED HOME CAUSE BLACK WAS HEADED TO HER HOUSE IN A HOUR BLACK ARRIVED A HOUR LATER HE HUNG OUT WITH KENEKA FOR A COUPLE HOURS THEN HE GOT READY TO LEAVE SHE DIDN'T WANT HIM TO GO BUT BEFORE HE LEFT SHE HANDED HIM A

KEY TO HER HOUSE HE TOOK IT AND
SAID WHATS THIS FOR WITH A
SURPRISED LOOK ON HIS FACE KENEKA
SAID SO YOU CAN GET IN WHEN EVER
YOU WANNA SHOW UP BLACK LOOKED
AT HER AND SAID OOOOK…..THANKS
KENEKA AND BLACK ENDED UP BACK
TOGETHER FOR ABOUT 7 MONTHS TOTAL
AROUND THE 3RD MONTH KENEKA WENT
TO WORK AND SHE STARTED FEELING
REAL DIZZIY AND NAUSEOUS KENEKA
WENT TO THE BATHROOM AND STARTED
THROWING UP SHE DIDN'T KNOW WHAT
WAS WRONG WITH HER SO HER BOOS
LETS HER LEAVE EARLY AND KENEKA
GOES TO THE HOSPITAL AFTER BEING

SEEN KENEKA FINDS OUT SHE WAS PREGNANT KENEKA WAS SO HAPPY SHE WANTED TO HAVE KIDS BY HIM AND BE HIS WIFE AS WELL LATER THAT EVENING BLACK CALLED KENEKA AND SAID HE WAS ON HIS WAY OVER KENEKA SAID OK SHE COULDN'T WAIT TO TELL HIM THE NEWS ABOUT 30 MINS LATER BLACK ARRIVED AT HER HOUSE HE COMES IN AND SITS DOWN KENEKA BEGINS TO SMILE AT HIM SHE DIDN'T REALIZE SHE WAS DOING IT AND BLACK SAID WHAT ! KENEKA REPLIED I GOT SOMETHING TO TELL YOU BLACK LOOKED AT HER WITH CONCERN ON HIS FACE AND SAID OK WHATS UP KENEKA REPLIED I AM

PREGNANT BLACK JUST LOOKED AT HER WITH NO EMOTION ON HIS FACE KENEKA REPLIED WHATS WRONG BLACK REPLIED NOTHING KENEKA REPLIED WHY DO YOU LOOK LIKE YOU DONT WANT A BABY BLACK REPLIED NO BABY I DO WANT THE BABY KENEKA REPLIED OK ... ABOUT 30 MINUTES LATER BLACK TOLD KENEKA HE HAD TO GO KENEKA REPLIED OK AND HE GAVE HER A KISS AND LEFT ABOUT 6 MONTHS LATER KENEKA AND BLACK WHERE STILL TOGETHER AND KENEKA WAS STARTING TO SHOW MORE BLACK WOULD STILL COME OVER AND HE WOULD RUB ON HER STOMACH AND KISS HER STOMACH BLACK WAS NOW

SHOWING THAT HE WAS HAPPY TO BE HAVING THE BABY BUT ABOUT A WEEK LATER KENEKA GOT A CALL FROM ANOTHER WOMEN SHE BEGIN TO TELL KENEKA BLACK WAS LEAVING WITH HER AND HE WAS WITH HER KENEKA KNEW ALREADY SO SHE WASN'T SURPRISED WHEN SHE FOUND OUT THE LADY THEN ASKED KENEKA ARE THEM YOUR HOUSE KEYS HE GOT KENEKA REPLIED YES THEY ARE THEN KENEKA TOLD HER I AM 6 MONTHS PREGNANT WITH HIS SON THEN THE LADY REPLIED OH REALLY I WOULD GET A ABORTION IF I WAS YOU KENEKA REPLIED ITS TO LATER FOR THAT AND I AINT KILLING MY BABY BUT

YOU CAN HAVE HIM I AM GOOD THEN KENEKA HUNG UP AFTER KENEKA HUNG UP SHE BEGIN TO CRY VERY HARD SHE COULDN'T BELIEVE BLACK WAS CHEATING ON HER AGAIN AFTER GIVING HIM ANOTHER CHANCE ABOUT A MONTH LATER KENEKA GOT INTO SOME TROUBLE WITH THE LAW SHE WAS IN TROUBLE FOR SOME THEFT SHE DID SHE WAS TOLD BY HER NEIGHBOR THAT THE POLICE WAS THERE LOOKING FOR HER AND GAVE HER THE CARD THEY LEFT KENEKA SAID OK THANKS KENEKA WENT IN HER PLACE AND STARTED FREAKING OUT FIRST THING THAT CAME TO HER MIND WAS WHATS GOING TO HAPPEN TO

MY BABY KENEKA DIDN'T KNOW THAT IT WASN'T AS BAD AS SHE THOUGHT IT WAS THEN ALL OF A SUDDEN KENEKA GETS A CALL FROM BJ SHE WAS SURPRISED TO SEE HIM CALLING KENEKA ANSWERED BJ HEADED HER CRYING HE SAID WHY YOU CRYING WHATS GOING ON WITH YOU KENEKA SHE REPLIED THE COPS ARE LOOKING FOR ME BJ CUSSES AND SAY OK WELL YOU GOT TO LEAVE MINNESOTA I AM ON MY WAY START PACKING YOUR STUFF KENEKA REPLIES OK KENEKA PACKS UP AS MUCH AS SHE COULD FIT IN THE CAR KENEKA REALLY DIDN'T WANT BJ BACK AROUND HER BUT SHE NEEDED HELP BJ GOT TO HER HOUSE ABOUT 30

MINUTES LATER BJ SAID TO KENEKA
LEFT GO YOU GOING TO GO TO MY BOYS
HOUSE AND ILL COME BACK AND LOAD
THIS STUFF IN THE CAR CAUSE YOU DONT
NEED TO BE SITTING HERE ANY LONGER
BECAUSE THE COPS WILL COME BACK AT
ANYTIME KENEKA SAID OK LETS GO
THEY JUMP IN THE CAR AND BJ TAKES
HER TO HIS BOYS HOUSE ON THE OTHER
SIDE OF TOWN THEN BJ WENT BACK TO
GRAB EVERYTHING AND CAME BACK
ABOUT A HOUR LATTER THEY STAYED AT
BJ BOYS HOUSE FOR A COUPLE DAYS
THEN THE SECOND DAY WHEN KENEKA
WOKE UP AT BJ'S BOYS HOUSE
SOMETHING WAS TELLING HER TO LOOK

OUT THE WINDOW WHEN SHE LOOKED THERE WAS A TOW TRUCK BY HER CAR HE WAS GETTING READY TO TOW HER CAR KENEKA RAN OUT THE DOOR AND DOWN THE STAIRS KENEKA GOT TO HIM JUST AS HE WAS LIFTING IT UP SHE HAD TO PAY 60.00 DOLLARS FOR HIM TO PUT IT DOWN KENEKA SAID HERES THE MONEY NOW PUT MY CAR DOWN !!!! KENEKA DIDNT KNOW THEY HAD PEMIT PARKING AT BJ'S BOYS HOUSE AND SHE WAS GLAD SHE CAUGHT HIM BEFORE HE DROVE OFF WITH HER CAR THEN KENEKA MOVED HER CAR TO A SAFE SPOT AND WENT BACK UPSTAIRS WHEN KENEKA GOT BACK UPSTAIRS BJ WAS ON

THE PHONE WITH HIS FAMILY IN WAUKEGAN IL ONCE BJ GOT OFF THE PHONE HE TOLD KENEKA WE LEAVING WE GOING DOWN THERE WITH MY FAMILY KENEK SAID OK LETS GO KENEKA WAS SCARED AND DIDN'T KNOW IF THE POLICE WAS GOING TO TAKE HER BABY OR NOT SO SHE WAS READY TO GET OUT OF MINNESOTA SO THEY WENT TO THE CAR AND HIT THE HIGHWAY ABOUT 8 HOURS LATER THEY ARRIVED IN ILLINOIS THEY WENT TO HIS AUNTIES HOUSE THEY STAYED THERE FOR 2MONTHS THEN KENEKA WENT INTO LABOR KENEKA WAS IN LABOR FOR ABOUT 6HOURS ONCE KENEKA WNT IN

THE HOSPTAIL BJ CALLED HER MOM AND
HER MOM JUMPED ON THE NEXT BUS TO
GET DOWN THERE KENEKAS MOM
ARRIVED RIGHT BEFORE THE DOCTORS
ENDED UP HAVING TO DO A C SECTION
THE DOCTOR TOLD BJ HE HAD TO PUT
ONE OF THE DOCTOR SUITES ON SO BJ
WENT TO CHANGE INTO ON KENEKA WAS
IN PAIN HER MOM WAS HOLDING HER
HAND AND TRYING TO HELP HER
CONCENTRATE ON BREATHING WHEN BJ
CAME BACK OUT KENEKA BUSTED OUT
LAUGHING AND SAID YOU LOOK LIKE A
TELETUBBY BJ STARTED LAUGHING AND
REPLIED YOU GOT JOKES KENEKAS MOM
COULDN'T STOP LAUGHING THE OUTFIT

WAS SKIN TIGHT ON HIM AND HE WAS BIG SO HE LOOKED REAL CRAZY THE DOCTOR BEGIN TO LAUGH AT WHAT KENEKA SAID AS WELL THEN THE RUSH KENEKA TO HAVE A C SECTION DONE CAUSE SHE ONLY DILATED TO 8 SO SHE HAD TO GET A C SECTION ONCE KENEKA GOT TO THE AREA WHERE THEY DID IT THEY TOLD BJ WHAT EVER HE DO DONT STAND UP AND LOOK WHEN THEY CUT HER OPEN CAUSE HE WILL PASS OUT BJ REPLIED OK KENEKA STARTED GIVING VERY SCARED BJ HELD HER HAND AND TOLD HER SHE WAS GOING TO BE OK AFTER A FEW MINUTES KENEKA CLAIMED DOWN THE DOCTOR ASKED

KENEKA DO YOU FEEL ANYTHING
KENEKA SAID NO NEXT THING KENEKA
KNEW HER BABY STARTED CRYING HE
WAS OUT THEY SHOWED KENEKA HER
BABY HE LOOKED JUST LIKE KENEKA
WHILE THEY CLOSED KENEKA BACK UP
BJ WENT WITH THE BABY TO GET HIS
SHOTS KENEKA WAS SHIVERING FOR A
HOUR AND THEN FEEL A SLEEP ABOUT A
HOUR LATER AFTER THEY HAD KENEKA
ON WATCH THEY TOOK HER TO HER
ROOM WHEN KENEKA WOKE UP SHE
LOOKED AROUND AND SEEN BJ SITTING
THERE LOOKING AT HER KENEKA THEN
SAID WHERES MY BABY BJ REPLIED HES
IN THE NURSERY KENEKA PUSHED THE

NURSE BUTTON AND TOLD THE NURSE SHE WANTED HER BABY A FEW MINTUES LATER THEY CAME IN WITH HER BABY KENEKA JUST SAT THERE LOOKING AT HIM AND HOLDING HIM HE WAS SO CUTE KENEKA BEGIN TO THINK TO HER SELF I WISH BLACK WAS HERE FOR THE BIRTH OF HIS SON KENEKA STARTED FEELING GUILTY CAUSE SHE HAD TO LEAVE MINNESOTA SHE WANTED BLACK THERE WITH HER BJ WAS NOT HIS DAD AND KENEKA DIDN'T FEEL RIGHT THAT BJ WAS THERE AND NOT BLACK THE NEXT DAY BJ'S FAMILY SHOWED UP AT THE HOSPITAL WITH A CAR SEAT CLOTHES AND DIPPERS BECAUSE KENEKA DIDNT

HAVE NOTHING FOR THE BABY AT ALL
ONE OF BJ'S FAMILY MEMBERS SAID TO
BJ YOUR SON IS SO CUTE BJ SAID THANK
YOU KENEKAS FACE DID A 360 SHE WAS
FURIOUS SHE BEGIN TO STARE AT BJ , BJ
SEEN THE LOOK ON HER FACE AND SAID
WHAT KENEKA THEN REPLIED WILL
TALK LATER KENEKA DIDN'T WANT TO
GO OFF ON HIM IN FRONT OF HIS FAMILY
SO SHE WAIT TED CAUSE SHE WASN'T
GOING AND BJ LOOKED AT HER HE KNEW
SHE WAS GOING TO SNAP BJS FAMILY
STAYED IN THE HOSPITAL FOR ABOUT A
HOUR HOLDING THE BABY AND TALKING
TO KENEKA AND BJ THEN AFTER THEY
LEFT KENEKA WENT OFF SHE WAS

CUSSING AND GETTING LOUD THEN SHE
SAID WHO DO YOU THINK YOU ARE
TELLING YOUR FAMILY THIS IS YOUR
SON AND YOU KNOW HE AIN'T THIS IS
BLACKS BABY NOT YOURS I AIN'T BEEN
WITH YOU IN A YEAR SO WHY YOU
SITTING UP HERE LIEING TO THEM I
AIN'T JUST GOING TO SIT UP HERE AND
LET YOU THINK YOU GOING TO TAKE HIS
DADS PLACE CAUSE YOU AIN'T BLACK
WILL BE IN HIS SONS LIFE KNOW THAT
AND MY SON WILL KNOW THAT BLACK IS
HIS DAD YOU GOT ME AND BLACK
MESSED UP AND I WILL BE GOING BACK
TO MINNESOTA SO BLACK WILL SEE HIS
SON YOU GOT ME REAL MESSED UP

KENEKA GETS QUITE BJ JUST LOOKS AT HER AND DOESN'T SAY ANYTHING ... BJ'S PHONE STARTS RINGING HE ANSWERS IT SOON AS HE GETS OFF THE PHONE HE TELLS KENEKA ILL BE BACK IN A LITTLE BIT KENEKA JUST LOOKS AT HIM WITH A EVIL LOOK ON HER FACE AND CONTINUES ENJOYING HER BABY BJ WALKS OUT THE ROOM  ABOUT FIVE MINUTES AFTER BJ LEAVES THE NURSE COMES IN WITH PAPERS AND ASK KENEKA HAVE YOU DESIDED ON A NAME FOR THE BABY YET KENEKA REPLIES YES SHE WROTE HIS NAME DOWN ON THE PAPER SHE NAMED HIM   DE ANDRE DE ANTE HARRIS THE NURSE THEN TAKES

THE PAPER FORM KENEKA AND ASKED HER IF SHE NEEDED ANYTHING KENEKA REPLIED NO I AM OK THE NURSE SAYS OK AND WALKS OUT THE ROOM KENEKA WAS JUST SITTING THERE WITH DEANDRE AND THINKING ABOUT HOW BAD SHE WANTED BLACK TO BE WITH HER AT THAT MOMENT SHE BEGIN CRYING ABOUT A HOUR LATER BJ COMES BACK IN AND HE SEES THE COPY OF THE PAPER FROM KENEKA NAMING THE BABY HE PICKS IT UP AND LOOKS AT THEN HE SAYS TO KENEKA YOU NAMED HIM WHY COULDNT YOU WAIT I WANTED HIS NAME TO BE SOMETHING ELSE NOT DEANDRE KENEKA BEINGS TO CUSS AND SAYS THIS

AIN'T YOUR SON SO WHAT MAKES YOU THINK YOU WAS GOING TO HAVE ANYTHING TO DO WITH HIS NAME DIDN'T I JUST GET DONE SNAPPING ON YOU ABOUT CALLING HIM YOUR AND HE AIN'T DON'T MAKE ME GET OUT THIS BED I AIN'T PLAYING WITH YOU HE AIN'T YOURS !!!!!!! KENEKA WAS READY TO PUT HER HANDS ON BJ HE WAS REALLY PISSING HER OFF THEN NEXT THING KENEKA KNEW THE NURSE WALKED IN THE ROOM AND SAID IS EVERYTHING OK KENEKA REPLIED I AM SORRY YEAH EVERYTHING IS FINE THE NURSE SAID OOOOK….. AND WALKED BACK OUT THE DOOR ABOUT 2 DAYS LATER KENEKA

WAS RELEASED AND WAS ABLE TO LEAVE THEN BJ TOOK KENEKA BACK TO HIS AUNTIES HOUSE WHEN THEY GOT THERE BJ'S AUNTIE PULLED BJ TO THE SIDED NEXT THINK KENEKA KNOWS BJ COMES BACK AND TELLS HER THEY CANT STAY THERE ANYMORE SO BJ AND KENEKA LEAVE THEN BJ ASKS OTHER FAMILY AND EVERYONE STARTED ACTING FUNNY AT THE SAME TIME SO KENEKA WAS LIVING IN HER CAR FOR ABOUT A MONTH SHE WAS CUT WIDE OPEN FROM THE C SECTION AND SLEEPING IN THE CAR WITH A BABY KENEKA COULD NOT BELIEVE HOW EVIL BJ'S FAMILY GOT WITH HER SO AFTER

ABOUT A MONTH OF SLEEPING IN THE CAR BJ DRIVES TO KENOSHA WISCONSIN KENEKA FINIAL GOT A BREAK SHE FOND A SHELTER THAT WAS FOR WOMEN AND KIDS THEY TOOK HER IN IMMEDIATELY BUT BJ COULDN'T STAY THERE WITH HER SO HE HAD TO KEEP SLEEPING IN THE CAR KENEKA WAS THERE FOR ABOUT 2 WEEKS KENEKA WAS GOING THREW PTSD SHE WAS NOT EATING SINCE SHE GOT OUT THE HOSPITAL ALL SHE WOULD DO IS SMOKE CIGARETTES SHE WOULDN'T EAT OR DRINK NOTHING THIS WENT ON FOR A MONTH KENEKA GOT VERY SMALL SHE WAS LOSINGS WEIGHT LIKE CRAZY KENEKA STARED HAVING

PAIN IN HER STOMACH SO BJ TOOK HER INTO THE HOSPITAL WHEN THEY DID A EX RAY THEY SEEN THAT KENEKA HAD SOME GREEN STUFF IN HER SO THEY HAD TO PUT A TUBE IN HER THAT HAD TO STAY IN HER TILL THE GREEN STUFF DRAINED OUT KENEKA WAS ADMITTED TO THE HOSPITAL AFTER NOT EATING FOR OVER A MONTH AND NOW HAVING GREEN STUFF IN HER THAT CAUSED STOMACH PAIN ABOUT A WEEK LATER KENEKA WAS STILL IN THE HOSPITAL AND STILL WASNT EATING NOTHING BJ SAID TO KENEKA YOU ARE SCARING THE MESS OUT OF ME RIGHT NOW YOU NEED TO EAT SOMETHING KENEKA REPLIED I

AM NOT HUNGRY KENEKAS STOMACH
DIDN'T GROWL FOR FOOD FOR OVER A
MONTH SO SHE DIDN'T HAVE A DESIRE
TO EAT ANYTHING SHES WAS GOING
THREW ALL KINDS OF EMOTIONS AND
SHE KEPT THINKING ABOUT BLACK AND
WANTING HIM THERE KENEKA WAS
STILL IN LOVE WITH HIM REGARLESS OF
WHAT HE HAD DID SHE STILL HAD LOVE
FOR HIM AND IT WAS VERY DEEP WITH
ANY OTHER GUY KENEKA WOULD WALK
AWAY AND NOT WANT THEM ANY MORE
BUT WITH BLACK SHE NEVER FELT THAT
WAY SHE STILL WAS IN LOVE WITH HIM
SHE RELIZED SHE HAD UN CONDITIONAL
LOVE FOR BLACK KENEKA KNEW THERE

WAS SOMETHING ABOUT HIM WHEN SHE FIRST SEEN HIM BACK IN THE DAY SHE FEEL IN LOVE WITH HIM RIGHT AWAY AND SHES BEEN IN LOVE WITH HIM EVERY SINCE 1997 IT WAS NOW 2008 AND SHE STILL FOUND HER SELF THINKING OF HIM AND SHE WAS STILL DEEPLY IN LOVE WITH BLACK AND WANTED HIM IN HIS SONS LIFE THE NEXT WEEK THE DOCTOR CAME IN AND BROUGHT KENEKA SOME FOOD KENEKA SAT UP AND TRIED TO EAT SHE ATE A LITTLE BIT BJ GOT HAPPY AND SAID CAN YOU EAT SOME MORE FOR ME PLEASE KENEKA SAID I DONT WANT NOMORE BUT AT DINNER TIME KENEKAS STOMACH WAS

GROWLING FINALLY IT HAD BEEN OVER A MONTH SINCE HER STOMACH GROWLED SO WHEN DINNER CAME SHE ATE THE WHOLE THING BJ WAS EXCITED THE DOCTOR CAME IN AND HIS EYES GOT BIG HE SAID TO KENEKA WOW YOU ATE THE WHOLE PLATE KENEKA SMILED THE DOCTOR SAID ITS ABOUT TIME YOU WHERE SCARING ME THAT'S ALONG TIME TO GO WITH OUT EATING KENEKA SAID I DON'T KNOW WHY I WAS LIKE THAT I DIDN'T EVEN HAVE A DESIRE TO EAT ANYTHING AFTER MY SON CAME OUT AT ALL THE DOCTOR REPLIED WELL I AM GLAD YOU ARE BACK TO YOUR SELF NOW  KENEKA REPLIED ME TO IT WAS

SCARING ME TO THE NEXT WEEK KENEKA WAS RELEASED FROM THE HOSPITAL IN MILWAUKEE WISCONSIN AFTER KENEKA AND BJ LEFT BJ RAN INTO A OLD FRIEND HIS FRIEND STARTED TELLING HIM ABOUT THE JOB HE HAD TRAVELING AND HE GAVE BJ THE NUMBER TO TALK TO THE BOSS AFTER HIS FRIEND LEFT BJ CALLED THE NUMBER RIGHT AWAY THE BOSS ANSWERED RIGHT AWAY NEXT THING BJ KNOWS THE BOSS SAYS HE WANTS BJ TO START RIGHT AWAY AND ASK HIM HOW LONG IT WOULD TAKE HIM TO GET TO LINCOLN NEBRASKA BJ TOLD HIM THAT HE WAS CURRENTLY IN WISCONSIN BUT

THE BOSS SAID HE AS WILLING TO WAIT FOR BJ TO ARRIVE AND HE TOLD BJ HE WOULD GET PAYED CASH ANYWHERE FROM 800-1000 A DAY CASH BJ SAID BET WE ON ARE WAY SO KENEKA AND BJ HEADED DOWN SOUTH TO LINCOLN NEBRASKA ABOUT 24-36 HOURS LATER THEY ARRIVED IN LINCOLN NEBRASKA THEN BJ CALLED THE BOSS AND THE BOSS TOLD HIM TO COME TO THE RED ROOF INN AND GAVE HIM THE ADDRESS WHEN THEY ARRIVED THE BOSS PAYED FOR THERE ROOM AND BJ BEGIN TO WORK BJ WAS MAKING ABOUT 900 A DAY IN CASH KENEKA COULDN'T BELIEVE IT AFTER BJ'S FIRST DAY HE CAME BACK IN

AND SAID THIS IS GREAT NOW WE DON'T
NEVER HAVE TO GO BACK TO
MINNESOTA KENEKA LOOKED AT HIM
CRAZY SHE SEEN WHAT HE WAS ON SHE
WASN'T STUPID HE WAS TRYING TO KEEP
HER FROM GOING BACK TO MINNESOTA
WHERE BLACK WAS SO KENEKA HAD A
PLAN SHE WAS NOT GOING FOR IT SO
SOON AS BJ WENT IN THE SHOWER SHE
SEACHED HIS POCKETS AND PULLED OUT
A BUNCH OF MONEY SO KENEKA TOOK
100.00 OUT EVERYDAY AND PUT IT TO THE
SIDE FOR HER SHE DID THIS EVERYDAY
WHEN BJ CAME IN FROM WORK THEY
ENDED UP GOING TO 11 OTHER STATES
BECAUSE THE JOB REQUIRED

TRAVELING BUT BJ DIDN'T GET PAID FOR
TRAVELING JUST WHEN HE COMPLETED
A JOB  BUT KENEKA WAS STILL
STACKING SHE DIDN'T CARE PLUS HE
WAS GETTING SO MUCH MONEY THEY HE
DIDN'T EVEN NOTICE SHE WAS TALKING
IT THAT'S HOW MUCH MONEY HE HAD A
DAY THEN AFTER GOING TO 10 OTHER
STATES THEY ENDED UP IN AUSTIN TEXES
THAT WAS THE 11TH STATE AND THE
BOSS PAYED FOR ALL HIS WORKERS
HOTELS IN EVERY STATE THEY WENT TO
SO THEY DIDN'T HAVE TO WORRY ABOUT
A PLACE TO STAY SO THEY GOT ALL
SETTLED IN AND BJ WENT TO WORK HIS
SHIFT THAT MORNING KENEKA AND HER

BABY WAS CHILLING AT THE HOTEL ONCE BJ LEFT KENEKA PULLED OUT ALL THE MONEY SHE HAD BEEN STASHING AND COUNTED IT SHE WAS AT 2,400 KENEKA STARTED LAUGHING AND SAID TO HER BABY BJ THINK HE GOING TO KEEP US AWAY FROM MINNESOTA AND YOUR DAD BUT GUESS WHAT NO HE AINT MOMMA GOT A PLAN BABY  DEANDRE ACTED LIKE HE KNEW WHAT SHE WAS SAYING BECAUSE SOON AS SHE WAS DONE TALKING DEANDRE STARTED LAUGHING AND KICKING HIS LITTLE FEET KENEKA WAS ROLLING SO SHE SAID IT TO HIM AGAIN MOMMA GOT A PLAN BABY DEANDRE STARTED LAUGHING AND

KICKING HIS LITTLE FEET AGAIN
KENEKA WAS LAUGHING SO HARD HER
STOMACH WAS HURTING DEANDRE WAS
REALLY GETTING A KICK OUT OF WHAT
SHE WAS SAYING AT THIS TIME DEANDRE
WAS 8 MONTHS OLD LATER ON THAT
EVENING BJ CAME BACK IN FROM WORK
AND WENT AND GOT IN THE SHOWER
SOON AS HE GOT IN THE SHOWER
KENEKA COUNTED WHAT HE MADE FOR
THE DAY IT WAS 1000 SO KENEKA TOOK
200.00 AND PUT IT BACK IN HIS PACKET
AND HURRYED UP AND STASHED IT
BEFORE HE CAME OUT THE SHOWER
KENEKA KEPT UP THE SAME THING FOR
THE NEXT 3 WEEKS STASHING EVERYDAY

HE CAME IN KENEKA WAS NOW AT 4,700
AND SHE WAS STILL GOING ANOTHER
WEEK PAST KENEKA WAS NOW AT 5,400
BUT THIS TIME WHEN BJ CAME IN FROM
WORK HE TOOK HIS CLOTHES OFF IN
THE BATHROOM HE WAS CATCHING ON
TO KENEKA IT TOOK HIM A WHILE BUT
THAT STILL DIDN'T STOP KENEKA SOON
AS SHE COULD TELL HE WAS IN THE
SHOWER KENEKA CHEEPED IN THE
BATHROOM REAL SLOW AND SEEN HIS
PANTS HANGING ON THE BACK OF THE
BATHROOM DOOR SO SHE REACHED IN
HIS POCKET AND GRABBED 2 MORE 100
DOLLAR BILLS BJ DIDN'T EVEN SEE HER
COME IN NOW SHE WAS AT 5,600 WHEN BJ

CAME OUT THE BATHROOM HE SAT
DOWN AND SAID TO KENEKA I AM
LOOKING THIS JOB AND I AM MAKING
GOOD MONEY KENEKA REPLIED YEAH
WE ARE MAKING GOOD MONEY BJ
LOOKED AT HER AND SAID WHAT YOU
TALKING ABOUT KENEKA SAID NOTHING
YOU MAKING GOOD MONEY BJ REPLIED
YEAH OK THEN BJ KEPT TALKING AND
SAID TO KENEKA WE GOING TO STAY
RIGHT HERE IN TEXTS WE DON'T NEED
TO GO BACK TO MINNESOTA KENEKA
THEN REPLIED OH NO WE AINT I AM
GOING BACK HOME WITH OR WITH OUT
YOU THATS MY CAR PARKED OUT THERE
NOT YOURS SO EITHER YOU GOING BACK

WITH ME OR ME AND DRE WILL GET THERE ON ARE OWN  I ALREADY LOOKED IT UP AND KNOW HOW TO GET BACK 35W STRAIGHT TO MINNESOTA YOU BETTER STOP PLAYING WITH ME YOU WILL GET LEFT HERE ILL LEAVE WHILE YOU GONE AT WORK SAY I WONT !!!! BJ JUST LOOKED AT HER FOR A SECOND KENEKA WAS A WOMEN WITH A PLAN SHE HAD PLENTY MONEY ON HER NOW SO IF SOMETHING HAPPEND TO HER CAR ON THE WAY BACK SHE WOULD STILL BE ABLE TO JUMP ON THE BUS OR GET IT REPAIRED HE WASN'T KEEPING HER FROM GETTING BACK TO MINNESOTA WHERE BLACK WAS SHE WAS NOT

PLAYING SO THEN BJ FINALLY REPLIED OK JUST LET ME FINNISH OUT THE WEEK AND THEN WE WILL LEAVE KENEKA SAID YEAH THAT'S WHAT I THOUGHT !!! SO BJ FINISHED OUT THE WEEK AND KENEKA DECIDED TO BE NICE AND NOT STASH ANY MORE HIM MONEY SHE HAD PLENTY BY THIS TIME WHEN SATURDAY MORNING CAME THEY HIT THE HIGHWAY AND HEADED BACK TO MINNESOTA IT TOOK THEM ABOUT 3 DAYS TO GET BACK TO MINNESOTA SOON AS KENEKA SEEN THE SKY SCRAPER OF DOWNTOWN MPLS SHE SCREAMED YES I AM HOME SHE STARTED DANCING AND SINGING MPLS ,MPLS MPLS WOOT WOOT

BJ LOOKED AT HER WITH A MAD LOOK
ON HIS FACE KENEKA SAID TO HIM I
DON'T CARE IF YOU MAD IT WAS EITHER
COME WITH OR GET LEFT YOU COULD OF
STAYED THERE I DIDN'T CARE THIS MY
CAR SO YOU HAD TO ROLL WITH OE GET
LEFT KENEKA STARTED LAUGHING IN
HIS FACE BJ JUST LOOKED AT HER WITH
A EVIL LOOK AND KEPT DRIVING SO BJ
HEADED OVER NORTH TO HIS SISTERS
HOUSE WHEN THEY GOT THERE KENEKA
CALLED THE POLICE TO SEE IF THERE
WAS A WARRENT OUT FOR HER AND
THEY TOLD HER THAT THERE WAS AND
KENEKA SAID TO THEM WHY IT TAKE
THEN SO LONG TO PUT A WARRANT  ON

ME THEY WAITED 6 MONTHS BEFORE THEY EVEN ISSUED A WARRANT FOR HER THE POLICE TOLD HER THEY WERNT SURE KENEKA REPLIED OK THANKS YOU SOON AS KENEKA HUNG UP BJ SAID IT TOOK THEM SO LONG CAUSE THEY DIDN'T HAVE NOTHING ON YOU THEN KENEKA LOOKS AT HIM AND SAYS THEN IF THATS THE CASE WHY YOU HAD ME ON THE RUN LIKE I KILLED SOMEBODY AND WHY EVERYTIME WE RAN INTO POLICE YOU ACTED LIKE THEY WAS COMING FOR ME AND SCARING ME KENEKA SAID OOOOH I KNOW WHY YOU WAS JUST TRYING TO USE THAT TO GET ME OUT OF TOWN AND GET ME TO THE

POINT WHERE I WOULDN'T COME BACK WELL GUESS WHAT IT DIDN'T WORK I AM GOING TO TURN MY SELF IN AND BLACK WILL BE SEEING HIS SON KNOW THAT !!!! BJ DIDN'T SAY ANYTHING HE JUST LOOKED AT HER KENEKA HAD FIGURED HIM OUT SO THEY STAYED AT BJS SISTERS HOUSE FOR FOR THAT WEEK THE NEXT MORNING KENEKA HAD BJ KEEP DRE WHILE SHE WENT TO GET SOME BRAIDS IN HER HAIR AND SHE ALSO HAD TO LOAD ALL HER MONEY ON A DEBIT CARD BEFORE SHE TURNED HER SELF IN SO KENEKA LEFT TO DO THAT SHE GOT BACK LATER THAT EVENING BJ SAID HOW DID YOU HAVE MONEY TO GET

YOUR HAIR DONE KENEKA REPLIED
CAUSE I DO MIND YOUR BUSINESS THATS
HOW AND KENEKA BEGIN LAUGHING BJ
JUST LOOKED AT HER KENEKA STARTED
LAUGHING AGAIN ABOUT 2 DAYS LATER
KENEKA TURNED HER SELF IN WHILE BJ
KEPT THE BABY SHE WAS THERE OVER
NIGHT AND SEEN THE JUDGE THE NEXT
MORNING THEY ENDED UP OFFERING
HER A PLEA DEAL AND GAVE HER
COMMUNITY SERVICE AND 3 YEARS
PROBATION WITH NO JAIL TIME KENEKA
WAS RELIEVED BJ HAD HER THINKING
SHE WAS GOING TO PRISON WITH WHAT
HE KEPT TELLING HER THEY RELEASED
KENEKA THEN KENEKA HEADED BACK

TO THE NORTH SIDE SHE FELT SO STUPID
8 MONTHS ON THE RUN FOR NOTHING
BECAUSE SHE WAS SCARED HER BABY
WAS GOING TO GET TAKEN FROM HER
AND BJ DIDN'T HELP WITH WHAT HE WAS
SAYING HE JUST MADE HER MORE
SCARED SO KENEKA COMM PLEATED
HER COMMUNITY SERVICE NOW ALL SHE
HAD LEFT WAS BEING ON PROBATION
FOR 3 YEARS AND SHE WAS DONE THE
NEXT WEEK KENEKA CALLED BJ AND
LET HIM KNOW SHE WAS BACK SO HE
COULD SEE HIS SON THE NEXT DAY HE
MET UP WITH KENEKA AT A PIZZA PLACE
KENEKA WAS HAPPY DRE WAS GOING TO
FINNALY SEE HIS DAD AND KENEKA WAS

ALSO HAPPY THAT SHE WAS GOING TO SEE HIM TO WHEN BLACK ARIVED HE SAT DOWN AT THE TABLE AND ASK KENEKA HOW YOU DOING KENEKA SAID I AM OK AND HANDED HIM DE ANDRE KENEKA WAS FILLED WITH JOY WAS SHE WATCHED BLACK HOLDING HIS SON ITS WHAT SEE HAD BEEN WANTING EVER SINCE DRE WAS BORN THEN KENEKA NOTICES A WEDDING RING ON HIS HAND AND SHE SAYS YOU GOT MARRIED BLACK REPLIES YEAH ... KENEKA REPLIED OH OK AND GOT QUITE THAT HURT HER CAUSE THAT WAS WHAT SHE WANTED WITH BLACK BUT HE PUT THE RING ON THE WOMEN THAT KEPT CHEATING ON

HIM AND THAT DIDN'T LOVE HIM INSTEAD BUT KENEKA KNEW THE MARRIAGE WASN'T GOING TO LAST CAUSE THE GIRL WAS NOT WIFE MATERIAL IN THE FIRST PLACE AND SHE DIDN'T REALLY LOVE HIM THAT'S WHY DE ANDRE ENDED UP BEING MADE IN THE FIRST PLACE BUT BLACK WAS STILL BLIND FAR AS KENEKA WAS CONCERNED BUT KENEKA STILL WANTED HIM BACK SHE DIDNT UNDERSTAND WHY BECAUSE WHEN OTHER MEN HURT HER SHE COULD LEAVE THEM WITH NO PROBLEM WHEN SHE WAS DONE SHE WAS DONE BUT IT WASN'T LIKE THAT WITH BLACK FOR SOME REASON KNEKA HAD UN

CONDITIONAL LOVE FOR BLACK AND

AND WAS VERY DEEP ... ABOUT 30 MINS

LATER BLACK HANDS HER DRE BACK

AND SAYS I GOTTA GO ILL CALL YOU

KENEKA REPLIES OK AND BLACK LEAVES

KENEKA PUTS BACK ON DE ANDRES COAT

AND PUTS HIM BACK IN HIS STROLLER

AND HEADS BACK TO THE NORTH SIDE OF

MPLS  BLACK STARTED TO CALL KENEKA

TO SEE HIS SON MORE SHE WAS HAPPY

ABOUT THAT PART ABOUT 3 MONTHS

LATER KENEKA MESSED WITH BJ AGAIN

AFTER SEEING BLACK WAS MARRIED

ABOUT 2 WEEKS LATER KENEKA WASN'T

FEELING RIGHT AND WENT TO THE

DOCTOR SHE FOUND OUT SHE WAS NOW

PREGNANT WITH BJ'S BABY ONCE KENEKA GOT ALONG FAR ENOUGH SHE GOT HER FIRST ULTRASOUND AS THE LADY WAS LOOKING SHE SAID OMG KENEKA SAID WHAT ??? THE LADY REPLIED I SEE TWO HEADS YOUR HAVING TWINS ITS A BOY AND A GIRL KENEKA SCREAMED WHAT!!!!! THE LADY SAID IT AGAIN YOUR HAVING TWINS ISN'T THAT GREAT KENEKA SAID YEAH ... BUT SHE WASN'T HAPPY ABOUT IT THE LADY TOLD KENEKA SHE WAS GOING TO STEP OUT AND GET HER PICTURES AND SHE WOULD BE RIGHT BACK SOON AS THE LADY WALKED OUT KENEKA BEGIN TO CRY BECAUSE SHE KNEW SHE WAS

GOING TO HAVE TOO RAISE THEM BY
HER SELF CAUSE BJ COULDN'T EVEN
TAKE CARE OF HIS LET ALONE 2 BABYS
KENEKA WAS NOT HAPPY TO BE
PREGNANT BY HIM AT ALL BUT SHE
WASN'T KILLING HER BABYS SO 9
MONTHS LATER SHE WAS SCHEDULED TO
INDUCE HER LABOR BECAUSE HER BABY
BOY WAS TAKING ALL THE FOOD FROM
HER BABY GIRL SO KENEKA WENT IN TO
LABOR HER BOY CAME OUT FIRST BUT
HER GIRL WAS BUTT FIRST SO THEY HAD
TO TURN THE BABY AROUND AND SHE
STILL WOULDN'T COME OUT SO KENEKA
HAD TO HAVE ANOTHER SECTION
KENEKAS DAUGHTER HAD TO GET PUT IN

THE ICU BECAUSE SHE WAS 4 POUNDS 4OUNCES AND WASN'T HOLDING HER OWN HEAT SO KENEKA WAS IN THE HOSPITAL ABOUT A WEEK AFTER DELIVERING THEN WAS ABLE TO GO HOME CAUSE HER DAUGHTER WAS GOING BETTER THEN ABOUT A WEEK AFTER GOING HOME HER DAUGHTER WASN'T HOLDING HER OWN HEAT AGAIN SO KENEKA HAD TO GO BACK TO THE HOSPITAL THEY KEPT HER FOR ABOUT ANOTHER 2 WEEKS KENEKA STAYED THERE WITH HER THEN AFTER 2 WEEKS WENT BY SHE WAS DOING BETTER AND SHE WAS RELEASED AS TIME WENT ON KENEKA WAS DOING EVERYTHING HER

SELF BJ WASNT HELPING HER WITH NOTHING EVEN WHEN HE WAS AROUND HE WAS LAZY KENEKA CHANGED THE KIDS ALL THE TIME AND FEED THEM EVEY TIME THEY BABYS NEEDED TO BE CHANGED OR FEED BJ WOULD ALWAYS SAY KENEKA GET THEM WHEN HE WASN'T DOING NOTHING BUTT SITTING ON HIS FAT BUTT DOING NOTHING BUT STILL KEPT HAVING KENEKA DO EVERYTHING KENEKA KNEW HE WASN'T GOING TO HELP HER WITH NOTHING SHE ALREADY KNEW SHE WAS GOING TO HAVE TO DO EVERYTHING ON TOP OF DEALING WITH HIS ARGUING FOR NO REASON JUST LIKE HE ALWAYS DID IN

THE PAST SO WHEN 2012 HIT KENEKA FOUND OUT HE WAS CHEATING AND SHE DECIDED TO LEAVE HIM ALONE SHE WAS TIERED OF HIM ANY WAY SO SHE BROKE UP WITH HIM FOR GOOD THIS TIME SHE WANTED BLACK ANYWAY SO FOR THE NEXT YEAR KENEKA JUST STAYED SINGLE AND TOOK CARE OF HER BABYS SHE DIDN'T WANT TO BE BOTHER WITH A MAN PERIOD UNLESS IT WAS BLACK SHE WAS STILL THINKING ABOUT HIM HARD ... SO AFTER THE FIRST YEAR OF BEING SINGLE KENEKA GOT A CALL FROM BLACK HE WANTED TO COME OVER FOR HIS SONS BIRTHDAY KENEKA SAID OK SHE WAS DOING A LITTLE HOUSE PARTY

FOR HIM ANYWAY SO IT WORKED OUT PERFECT DEANDRE WAS TURNING 5 YEARS OLD IN A COUPLE DAYS AND SHE WAS SO GLAD BLACK WANTED TO SHOW UP FOR HIS BIRTHDAY TWO DAYS LATER KENEKA THREW THE PARTY AND BLACK SHOWED UP HE ATE FOOD WITH HIS SON AND HE ALSO CUT THE CAKE FOR THE FIRST TIME KENEKA WAS SO HAPPY BLACK STAYED FOR ABOUT AN HOUR KENEKA WAS TRYING NOT TO STARE AT BLACK TO MUCH THE WHOLE TIME HE WAS THERE ALL SHE COULD DO WAS THINK ABOUT HIM AND HER AND HOW MUCH SHE WANTED HIM BUT KENEKA KNEW SHE COULDN'T HAVE HIM AT THE

TIME SO SHE DID REAL GOOD AT NOT SHOWING THAT SHE WANTED HIM AND THAT SHE WAS STILL FEELING HIM BUT WHILE BLACK WAS TALKING WITH HIS SON KENEKA WAS STARRING AT BLACK AND BLACK CAUGHT HER HE TURNED AND LOOKED AT HER THEY LOCKED EYES FOR ABOUT A MINUTE THEN KENEKA GOT UP AND WENT BACK IN HER ROOM SHE WAS TRYING TO PLAY IT OFF BUT HE SEEN HER AFTER A FEW MINUTES SHE COMES BACK OUT AND GOES IN THE KITCHEN TO START CLEANING UP A LITTLE AS SHES CLEANING SHE SEES BLACK LOOKING AT HER SO SHE TURNS HER HEAD TO LOOK AT HIM TO THEY

LOCK EYES AGAIN FOR A FEW SECONDS THIS TIME AND KENEKA GOES BACK TO CLEANING THEN SHE SITS BACK DOWN IN THE LIVING ROOM AND STARTS PLAYING WITH HER PHONE CAUSE SHES TRYING NOT TO KEEP LOCKING EYES WITH BLACK BUT THEY CONTINUE TO KEEP LOCKING EYES ANYWAY ABOUT 20 MINUTES LATER BLACK SAYS HE HAS TO GO AND TOLD KENEKA HE WILL CALL HER KENEKA REPLIES OK BLACK GOES OUT THE DOOR AND KENEKA LOCKS THE DOOR BEHIND HIM THEN KENEKA PUTS HER BACK ON THE DOOR AND LOOKS DOWN KENEKAS MOM LOOKS AT KENEKA AND SAYS WHATS THAT ABOUT

KENEKA REPLIES MOM I STILL LOVE HIM I AM IN LOVE WITH HIM AND IT AIN'T NEVER WENT AWAY KENEKAS MOM REPLIES OH OK I THOUGHT SO  KENEKA LAUGHS AND STARTS CLEANING UP AND GETTING STUFF PUT AWAY THEN SHE TOOK HER MOM BACK HOME AND WENT BACK HOME FOR THE EVENING AND GOT THE KIDS READY FOR BED WHEN KENEKA LAY ED DOWN THAT EVENING ALL SHE COULD THINK ABOUT WAS BLACK KENEKA WAS CRAZY ABOUT BLACK SHE TOSSED AND TURNED TILL SHE FELL A SLEEP THAT NIGHT... BLACK KEPT IN CONTACT WITH KENEKA AND CONTINUED MAKING EFFORTS TO SEE

HIS SON A YEAR HAD PAST IT WAS NOW
2013 AFTER ABOUT A YEAR PASSING
KENEKA GET A CALL FROM BJ KENEKA
CANT BELIEVE HES CALLING HER SHE
HADN'T TALKED TO HIM IN A YEAR
KENEKA PICKS UP THE PHONE AND SAYS
WHAT !!! BJ REPLIES WHAT YOU MEAN
WHAT KENEKA REPLIES LIKE I SAID
WHAT !!! BJ REPLIES YEAH OK I NEED
YOUR HELP KENEKA REPLIES WITH
WHAT !!! BJ REPLIES I JUST GOT BACK
OFF THE ROAD AND I GOT FIRED AND I
NEED SOME WHERE TO STORE MY STUFF
KENEKA REPLIES OH REALLY YOUR GIRL
WONT HELP YOU WHY YOU CALLING ME
BJ REPLIES SHE AIN'T MY GIRL KENEKA

REPLIES WELL SHE WAS A YEAR AGO SO WHY CANT SHE HELP YOU BJ REPLIES COME ON KENEKA ... YOU STILL MAD ABOUT THAT REALLY ??? KENEKA REPLIES DONT GET IT TWISTED I AINT MAD THERE AINT A MAD BONE IN MY BODY FAR AS SHE GO I WANTED BLACK ANYWAY AND I TOLD YOU THAT SERVERL TIMES THATS WHY YOU KEPT GETTING MAD BACK IN THE DAY SO NO IT AIN'T ABOUT HER KEEP WISHING BJ REPLIES MAN FORGET WHAT YOU TALKING ABOUT AIN'T NO BODY SAY NOTHING ABOUT BLACK KENEKA REPLIES SEE YOU MAD BUT ANYWAY IF THAT'S YOUR GIRL I DON'T UNDERSTAND

WHY SHE CANT HELP YOU BJ GETS MAD AND REPLIES LOOK KENEKA CAN YOU PLEASE HELP ME KENEKA REPLIES YOU BETTER CHECK YOUR TONE OF VOICE WHEN YOU TALKING TO ME I DONT KNOW WHO YOU THINK YOU YELLING AT !!! BJ REPLIES OK I AM SORRY CAN YOU PLEASE HELP ME KENEKA REPLIES THATS BETTER YOU CAN PUT YOUR STUFF IN THE KIDS CLOSET BUT IT CANT BE HERE FOR EVER YOUR TIME IS LIMITED BJ REPLIES YEAH OK KENEKA GIVES BJ THE ADDRESS AND ABOUT 30 MINTUES LATER BJ SHOWS UP AND PUTS HIS STUFF IN THE KIDS CLOSET THEN BJ STARTS WITH KENEKA HE BEGIN TO SAY

SO YOU STUCK ON BLACK HUH HE AINT GOING TO COME BACK KENEKA REPLIES WHEN HE COMES TO HIS SINCE S YES HE WILL ME AND HIM GOT CHEMISTRY BJ LAUGHS AND REPLIES YEAH OK HOW MUCH YOU WANNA BET KENEKA REPLIES 200 BETTER YET HOW ABOUT 1000 THATS HOW MUCH I KNOW WHAT I AM TALKING ABOUT BJ JUST LOOKS AT HER AND SAYS NAW THATS OK NEVER MIND KENEKA REPLIES YEAH CAUSE YOU KNOW YOU WILL LOSES WITH YOUR JEALOUS SELF BJ GETS MAD AND CUSSES KENEKA STARTS LAUGHING AND REPLIES YOU CANT HANDLE THE TRUTH HUH I NEVER REALLY WANTED YOU YOU ONLY GOT A

CHANCE WITH ME CAUSE BLACK WALKED AWAY SO THE TRUTH IS THE TRUTH DEAL WITH IT NOW YOU CAN GET OUT MY HOUSE WITH ALL THE LOUD STUFF BJ JUST LOOKS AT KENEKA MEAN AND HEADS TO THE DOOR KENEKA REPLIES DON'T LET THE DOOR KNOB HIT YOU ON THE WAY OUT KENEKA CUSSES THEN SLAMS THE DOOR AND LOCKS IT A COUPLE DAYS LATTER BJ SENDS HER A TEXT SAYING HE WANNA SEE HIS KIDS KENEKA JUST LOOKS AT IT ... KENEKA HATES BEING AROUND BJ ALL HE DO IS START STUFF WITH HER ALL THE TIME ABOUT ANY AND EVERYTHING SO KENEKA HATED THAT SHE HAD KIDS BY

HIM SHE LOVES HER BABYS JUST HATES THAT THEY HAD TO BE BY HIM SO KENEKA THINKS ABOUT IT FOR ABOUT 5 MINUTES BEFORE SHE ANSWERED HIM BECAUSE HE WAS HOMELESS SO HE WOULD HAVE TO SIT UP IN HER HOUSE WITH THEM AND KENEKA REALLY DIDNT WANT TO BE BOTHERED WITH HIM WHAT SO EVER BUT SHE KNEW SHE HAD HIS KIDS SO SHE KINDA DIDN'T HAVE A CHOICE SO KENEKA REPLIES YEAH OK... SO EVERYTIME KENEKA LET HIM COME OVER SHE WOULD STAY IN HER ROOM AWAY FROM HIM CAUSE SHE DIDN'T WANT TO BE BOTHER AND WASN'T TRYING TO BE ARGUING OVER NOTHING

CAUSE THAT'S WHAT HE BE ON ... MANY DAYS KENEKA WISHED HER BIG BROTHER D WAS IN THE SAME STATE AS HER SO HE COULD GET ON BJ ABOUT MESSING WITH HER KENEKA HAD BEEN THREW SO MUCH EMOTIONAL AND MENTAL ABUSE FROM BJ KENEKA HAD MANY TIMES SHE WANTED TO GET AWAY FROM HIM BACK IN THE DAY SHE EVEN CRYED TO GOD ASKING HIM TO GET BJ AWAY FROM HER KENEKA WENT THREW ALOT OF BAD THINGS IN HER LIFE THAT HURT HER SHE WAS SO BAD AT ONE POINT THAT SHE CUT HER OWN RISK AND WAS IN THE PHYCH WARD FOR A WEEK KENEKA HAD BEEN THREW ALOT AND

NOW SHE WAS STUCK DEALING WITH BJ AND HIS BS SHE WAS TIRED SHE REALLY WANTED HER BROTHER AT THIS POINT IN HER LIFE CAUSE SHE KNOWS HE WILL PROTECT HER KENEKA COULD FIGHT SHE HAD SOME HANDS ON HER AND A MOUTH BUT KENEKA WAS TIRED OF FIGHTING … SO WHEN BJ WAS THERE SHE STAYED IN HER ROOM HE WOULD TRY AND CALL HER MANY TIMES HE WOULD YELL KENEKA!!! HEY KENEKA !!! BUT SHE WOULD IGNORE HIM CAUSE SHE ALREADY KNOW WHAT HE WAS ON AND HE CONTINUED TO DO THIS EVERY TIME HE CAME OVER TO SEE HIS KIDS WHILE THIS IS GOING ON KENEKA AND BLACK

WHERE STILL KEEPING IN TOUCH ABOUT A WEEK LATER BLACK TEXTS KENEKA AND SAYS HE WANTS TO STOP BY TO SEE HIS SON KENEKA GETS HAPPY SHE COULDN'T HELP IT SO KENEKA SAID OK I AM AT HOME ABOUT A HOUR LATER BLACK SHOWS UP HE SPENDS MORE TIME WITH HIS SON AND READS A BOOK WITH HIM WHEN BLACK WAS READY TO LEAVE KENEKA OFFERED TO GIVE HIM A RIDE BLACK LOOKS AT HER AND SAYS YOU KNOW YOU DON'T HAVE TO DO THAT RIGHT KENEKA REPLIES I WANT TO BLACK REPLIES OK I APPRECIATE IT SO KENEKA AND THE KIDS AND BLACK HEAD OUT TO THE CAR WHILE KENEKA IS

DRIVING BLACK ASKS KENEKA SO WHERES YOUR MAN AT KENEKA REPLIES I AIN'T GOT NO MAN BLACK REPLIES OH OK AS PRETTY AS YOU ARE I THOUGHT SOMEONE WOULD OF HAD YOU KENEKA REPLIES NO N APPROACH ME ALL THE TIME I JUST DON'T WANT TO BE BOTHERED PLUS THEY AIN'T WHAT I WANT ANYWAY BLACK LOOKS AT KENEKA IN SILENCE KENEKA LOOKS AT HIM BACK AND THEY LOCK EYES FOR A SECOND THEN THE LIGHT CHANGES SO KENEKA TURNED HER EYES BACK TO THE ROAD THEN BLACK REPLIES OH OK... BLACK THEN GETS QUITE AND SO DOES KENEKA AND THEY ARE NOW JUST

LISTENING TO THE MUSIC ON THE WAY TO DROP HIM BLACK OFF KENEKA GETS TO SUPER AMERICA IN SAINT PAUL WHERE BLACK WANTED TO GET DROPPED OFF AT BLACK BEGINS TO SPEAK WELL THANKS FOR THE RIDE I APPRECIATE IT KENEKA REPLIES YOUR WELCOME THEN BLACK TURNS AROUND AND TELLS DEANDRE ILL SEE YOU LATER SON THEN HE GETS OUT THE CAR AND KENEKA HEADS BACK HOME A COUPLE DAYS LATER BLACK CALLED KENEKA AND ASK HER TO COME GET HIM AND HE TOLD HER HE WAS DONE KENEKA WASN'T SURE WHAT HE WAS TALKING ABOUT BUT KENEKA REPLIED OK AND

GOT THE KIDS TOGETHER AND HEADED OUT TO GO GET BLACK ONCE KENEKA GOT BACK TO THE GAS STATION SHE DROPPED HIM OFF AT A COUPLE DAYS AGO SHE SAW BLACK AND HE HAD A BAG IN HIS HAND BLACK PUT HIS STUFF IN THE CAR ONCE HE GOT IN KENEKA COULD FEEL HIS ENERGY HE WAS VERY ANGRY AND KENEKA FELT EVERY BIT OF IT AND IT MADE HER FEEL UNCOMFORTABLE KENEKA BEGIN TO SPEAK SHE SAID WHATS WRONG ??? BLACK BEGIN TO SPEAK HE SAID I AM DONE WITH HER I TOLD HER IF SHE STAY OUT ALL NIGHT AGAIN I WAS DONE KENEKA SAID OH OK AND THEN KENEKA

AND BLACK WENT BACK TO HER HOUSE KENEKA AND BLACK TALKED FOR A WHILE KENEKA AND BLACK ENDED UP BACK TOGETHER AGAIN AFTER SO MANY YEARS OF BEING APART BLACK TOLD KENEKA I DON'T WANT YOU TO THINK I ONLY CAME BACK CAUSE SHE WASN'T DOING ME RIGHT WE WHERE GOING TO BE DONE EVEN IF I DIDN'T GET YOU BACK KENEKA REPLIED OK BLACK STAY AT HER HOUSE ALL DAY THEN WHEN IT BEGIN TO GET LATE HE ASKED KENEKA TO TAKE HIM TO THE SHELTER CAUSE HE KNEW HE COULDN'T STAY WITH HER BECAUSE SHE WAS IN A PLACE FOR WOMEN AND KIDS ONLY  KENEKA

REPLIED OK AND TOOK HIM BACK DOWN TO THE SHELTER WHEN THEY ARRIVED BLACK THANKED KENEKA FOR THE RIDE AND TOLD HER HE WOULD TALK TO HER SOON AND GAVE HER A KISS AND GOT OUT THE CAR THEN KENEKA HEADED BACK HOME KENEKA WAS SO HAPPY TO BE BACK WITH BLACK THAT'S ALL SHE WANTED SINCE 1997 WAS TO BE WITH HIM AND HAVE HIS KIDS AND BECOME HIS WIFE KENEKA WAS HOPING THINGS WOULD WORK OUT THIS TIME LIKE SHE ALWAYS WANTED IT ABOUT 6 MONTHS PAST KENEKA AND BLACK WHERE STILL TOGETHER AND DOING GOOD IT WAS NOW 2013 BLACK JUST GOT HIS NEW

PLACE HE WAS EXCITED ABOUT IT AND KENEKA WAS GLAD THAT HE GOT OUT THE SHELTER TO SO KENEKA AND BLACK SPENT A LOT MORE TIME TOGETHER KENEKA WOULD BE AT HIS HOUSE EVERY WEEKEND WHEN BLACKS BIRTHDAY CAME UP SHE GOT HIM A CAKE AND HAD A SMALL PARTY AT HIS HOUSE IT WAS HER THE KIDS AND BLACKS COUSIN THAT WAS THERE THE DAY AFTER HIS BIRTHDAY BLACK HAD A SEIZURE KENEKA BROKE DOWN CRYING AND CALLED THE POLICE THEY ARRIVED AND TOOK HIM TO THE HOSPITAL KENEKA WAS BEHIND THEM IN HER CAR WITH THE KIDS WITH HER KENEKA SAT AT THE

HOSPITAL WITH HIM UP TO 1030 THAT NIGHT BUT KENEKA COULD NOT SIT IN THE HOSPITAL WITH HIM BECAUSE SHE HAD THE KIDS WITH HER SHE DIDN'T REALLY WANT TO LEAVE HIS SIDE AT ALL BUT SHE DECIDED TO GO BACK TO HIS HOUSE INSTEAD OF GOING ALL THE WAY BACK HOME CAUSE KENEKA STAYED 15 MILES AWAY FROM HIM SO SHE GOT THE KIDS AND WENT BACK TO HIS HOUSE FOR THE NIGHT SHE COULDN'T REALLY SLEEP CAUSE SHE WAS SO WORRIED ABOUT HIM  THE NEXT MORNING SHE GOT UP EARLY AND GOT THE KIDS BREAKFAST AND RUSHED BACK TO THE HOSPITAL ABOUT 30 MINUTES

AFTER SHE GOT THERE THE DOCTORS WHERE GETTING READY TO WAKE HIM UP CAUSE THEY HAD HIM ON A MED THAT KEPT HIM SLEEPING SO HE WOULD RELAX WHEN HE WOKE UP HE LOOKED SURPRISED WHEN HE SEEN KENEKA AND THE KIDS SITTING THERE DE ANDRE SAID HI DAD HE SAID HI SON THEN BLACK SAID TO KENEKA I HAD A SEIZURE KENEKA REPLIED YES YOU DID THEN THE DOCTOR CAME IN THE ROOM AND TALKED TO BLACK AND TOLD HIM HE WAS GOING TO GET RELEASED ABOUT 30 MINUTES LATER THEY HEAD BACK TO KENEKAS CAR THEN THEY GO BACK TO BLACKS HOUSE ABOUT 2 MONTHS LATER

AUGUST 2013 KENEKA AND BLACK HAD A DISAGREEMENT  AND KENEKA ENDED UP LEAVING BLACK KENEKA DIDN'T HANDLE ARGUING VERY WELL SHE WAS DAMAGED FROM ALL THAT ARGUING SHE DID WITH BJ SO ALL SHE KNEW HOW TO DO WAS RUN CAUSE THAT'S WHAT SHE DID FOR MANY YEARS DEALING WITH BJ KENEKA DIDN'T WANT TO BE ARGUING AGAIN SHE HAD MORE THAN ENOUGH OF THAT FROM BJ AND SHE DIDN'T WANT TO GO THREW IT AGAIN BUT HER LOVE FOR BLACK WAS TILL THERE LIKE IT HAS ALWAYS BEEN SHE JUST DIDN'T HANDLE ARGUING VERY WELL ANYMORE BUT 2 MONTHS LATER

ON HER BIRTHDAY KENEKA AND BLACK
ENDED UP BACK TOGETHER THEY WENT
OUT TO A MOVE FOR HER BIRTHDAY AND
MADE UP ABOUT 2 YEARS LATER KENEKA
AND BLACK WHERE STILL TOGETHER
THEY WHERE STILL GOING THREW THE
ON AND OFF BECAUSE KENEKA DIDN'T
KNOW HOW TO DEAL WITH ARGUING
SHE WAS DAMAGED FROM ALL THE
ARGUING AND FIGHTING SHE DID WITH
BJ SO SHE WAS QUICK TO WANNA GET
AWAY AND AVOID ARGUING BUT THREW
IT ALL KENEKA STILL LOVED BLACK
THAT'S SOMETHING THAT NEVER
TURELY WENT AWAY FOR KENEKA IT
WAS NOW FEBRUARY 2015 KENEKA AND

BLACK STILL HAD ARGUMENTS KENEKA WAS WONDERING WHY IT WAS GOING ON AND KENEKA ALSO NOTICE BLACK WASN'T HOW HE USE TO BE BACK IN THE DAY SOMETHING HAD CHANGED SHE JUST WASN'T SURE WHAT ... BECAUSE HER AND BLACK NEVER ARGUED NOW THEY DO IT WAS HARD FOR KENEKA TO DEAL WITH BUT SHE STILL WAS IN LOVE WITH HIM SO SHE KEPT TRYING DESPITE HER RUNNING OFF BECAUSE SHE COULDN'T HANDLE THE ARGUING SHE STILL FOUND HER SELF COMING BACK AT SOME POINT BECAUSE THREW IT ALL SHE WAS STILL IN LOVE WITH HIM ONE DAY HER AND BLACK WHERE TALKING

AND BLACK SAID TO HER I THINK WE NEED TO START GOING TO CHURCH BLACK WANTED TO SO KENEKA AGREED SO THEY STARTED GOING TO KENEKAS CHURCH EVERY SUNDAY AND THEY DIDN'T MISS ONE SUNDAY THEY WENT FAITHFULLY ABOUT 2 MONTHS AFTER THEY STARTED GOING TO CHURCH KENEKA AND BLACK STARTED GOING TO PARENTING AND HEALTHY RELATIONSHIP CLASSES AFTER 8 WEEKS OF GOING TO THE CLASSES KENEKA AND BLACK GRADUATED THE CLASSES BUT THEY STILL KEPT GOING ANYWAY BECAUSE THEY REALLY ENJOYED THE CLASSES AND IT WAS HELPING THEM AS

WELL KENEKA REALLY LOVED THE PARENTING CLASS SHE ADMIRED THE PERSON WHO WAS TEACHING THE CLASS AND THOUGHT TO HER SELF HE WOULD BE A GOOD FATHER FIGURE FOR ME HE WAS THE BOSS OF MAD DADS BUT HE DID THE PARENTING CLASSES EVERY TUESDAY AT URBAN VENTURES CENTER FOR FATHERING KENEKA WANTED HER FATHER AND WISH HE WOULD OF NEVER GO SHOT BEFORE SHE TURNED A YEAR OLD SO DEEP DOWN INSIDE KENEKA WANTED SOMEONE TO CALL DAD THAT WAS REALLY GOING TO BE A FATHER TO HER SHE HAD MEN IN AND OUT HER LIFE THAT HER MOM WAS DATING BUT SHE

DIDN'T SEE ANY OF THEM AS A FATHER FIGURE EVEN WHEN HER MOM GOT MARRIED SHE WOULD NOT CALL HIM DAD BECAUSE SHE WASN'T FEELING HIM AND HE WASN'T A FATHER FIGURE TO HER SO SHE WOULD ALWAYS CALL HIM BY HIS NAME SHE DIDN'T CARE AND DIDN'T REALLY WANT HER MOM TO MARRY HIM IN THE FIRST PLACE KENEKA HAD SEEN THIS GUY FROM MAD DADS ON SOCIAL MEDIA AND ON THE NEWS ALL THE TIME BUT THIS WAS THE FIRST TIME SHE GOT TO SEE HIM IN PERSON AND SEE HOW HE WAS KENEKA AND BLACK KEPT GOING TO THE GROUP FOR A WHOLE YEAR SO BY THIS TIME

KENEKA HAD REALLY GOTTEN TO KNOW THE PARENTING TEACHER AND BOSS OF MAD DADS  KENEKA WAS BEGINNING TO LOOK AT HIM AS FAMILY THERE RELATIONSHIP WAS GROWING HE WOULD EVEN TALK TO HER ON GLIDE AND FACEBOOK WHEN THERE WAS GROUP HE WOULD CHECK ON HER ALL THE TIME AND ASK HER HOW SHE WAS DOING AFTER A YEAR BLACK DIDN'T WANT TO GO TO THE GROUPS ANYMORE BUT KENEKA KEPT GOING BECAUSE SHE ENJOYED THEM ABOUT 4 MONTHS LATER A COUPLE DAYS BEFORE FATHERS DAY KENEKA WAS GOING THREW IT ABOUT NOT HAVING A DAD AND NOT KNOWING

WHAT IT WAS LIKE TO BE DADDY'S GIRL
SHE WAS CRYING AND DEPRESSED ALL
HER LIFE SHE NEVER HAD ANYONE TO
LOOK UP TO AS A FATHER AND SHE
DIDN'T HAVE HER BIOLOGICAL FATHER
EITHER SO KENEKA WAS ON SOCIAL
MEDIA TALKING ABOUT IT AND ABOUT 20
MINUTES AFTER SHE POSTED
SOMETHING ABOUT IT THE BOSS FROM
MAD DADS SENT HER A MESSAGE IN HER
INBOX AND ASKED HE WHAT WAS GOING
ON SHE TOLD HIM EVERYTHING ABOUT
WHAT HAPPENED TO HER FATHER
BEFORE SHE TURNED 1 YEAR OLD AND
HOW FOR MANY YEARS FATHERS DAY
WAS BAD FOR HER SHE WOULD CRY

EVERY TIME FATHERS DAY CAME UP AND ON REGULAR DAYS AS WELL BECAUSE DEEP DOWN SHE STILL HAD A DESIRE TO HAVE A FATHER OR SOMEONE WHO IS A FATHER FIGURE TO HER THEN HE TOLD HER YOU HAVE A FATHER NOW ILL BE YOUR GOD DAD WOULD YOU LIKE THAT KENEKA REPLIED YES THEN HE SAID OK WELL NOW YOU GOT A FATHER FIGURE IN YOUR LIFE  KENEKA FELT GOOD ABOUT IT BUT IT TOOK HER A WHILE BEFORE SHE STARTED CALLING HIM DAD SHE HAD BEEN CALLING HIM BY HIS NAME FOR A YEAR SO SHE HAD TO GET USE TO CALLING HIM DAD AND SHE ALSO HAD TO ADJUST TO SAYING DAD

CAUSE SHE HADN'T SAID DAD TO ANYONE FOR MANY YEARS SO AS TIME WENT ON SHE WOULD SAY IT EVERY NOW AND THEN BUT SHE FELT WEIRD WHEN SHE SAID DAD CAUSE SHE NEVER HAD THAT IN HER LIFE OR ANYONE TO CALL THAT AT THE END OF THAT MONTH AFTER FATHERS DAD HER GOD DADS BIRTHDAY WAS ON JUNE 26TH SO SHE WENT AND GOT HIM A CAKE FOR HIS BIRTHDAY WITH HIS PICTURE ON IT WITH THE MAD DAD COLORS ON THE CAKE AND SURPRISED HIM ON HIS BIRTHDAY HE LOVED IT AS TIME WENT ON KENEKA GOT MORE AND MORE USE TO CALLING HIM DAD AND AS TIME WENT ON SHE

ALSO NOTICE THAT HIS ACTIONS WHERE THAT OF A FATHER FIGURE HE CHECKED ON HER REGULARLY HE TOLD HER HE LOVED HER REGULARLY AND HE WOULD HUG HER AND KISS HER ON THE CHEEK AND PRAY FOR HER AND WHEN SHE WAS DOWN HE WAS THE ONE THAT WAS THERE FOR HER HE TALK WITH HER ABOUT EVERYTHING AND GOT ON HER ABOUT CRETIN STUFF AND TALKED TO HER ABOUT THINGS SHE COULD DO BETTER ON HE WAS VERY SUPPORTIVE IN ALL AREAS SO SEEING ALL THAT KENEKA KNEW HE WAS THE PERFECT FATHER FIGURE FOR HER SHE WAS GLAD SHE WAS GOING TO HIS PARENTING

CLASSES AND GOT TO MET HIM AND
BUILD A RELATIONSHIP WITH HIM
KENEKA KEPT GOING TO THE CLASSES
BUT WHEN DECEMBER 2016 CAME THEY
REPLACED HER GOD DAD WITH
SOMEONE NEW KENEKA WAS MAD AS
EVER THAT THEY LET HIM GO IT
BOTHERED KENEKA SO MUCH THAT SHE
STOPPED GOING TO THE PARENTING
CLASSES CAUSE IT WASN'T THE SAME
SHE LIKED THE WAY HER GOD DAD WAS
TEACHING IT SO SHE STOPPED GOING TO
PARENTING CLASSES AFTER THEY LET
HIM GO BUT KENEKA KEPT GOING TO
CHURCH AND SHE WAS STILL WITH
BLACK THINGS KEPT BEING SHAKY WITH

BLACK BUT SHE WAS STILL IN LOVE WITH HIM REGARDLESS ABOUT 2 MONTHS PAST IT WAS NOW FEBRUARY 2017 KENEKA WAS IN A VERY DEEP DEPRESSION AND SHE FOUND OUT HER VITAMIN D LEVEL WAS ONLY 9 SHE HAD WENT TO THE DOCTOR TO TRY AND FIGURE OUT WHAT WAS GOING ON CAUSE SHE WAS AT HER LOWEST SHE WAS NOT MOVATED TO DO ANYTHING SHE ISOLATED HER SELF A LOT SHE STOPPED WORKING HER BUSINESS WITH MCA SHE WENT FROM ADVERTISING AND HANDING OUT FLIERS EVERY DAY TO DOING NOTHING AND SITTING IN THE HOUSE IN HER ROOM IN BED ALL DAY

SHE KNEW SOMETHING WAS REALLY
WRONG SO SHE FOUND OUT THE A VERY
LOW LEVEL OF VITAMIN D CAN CAUSE
DEPRESSION TO GET BAD OR EVEN
WORSE IF YOU ALREADY HAVE IT SO THE
DOCTOR GAVE HER 50,000 OF VITAMIN D
TO TAKE ONCE A WEEK KENEKA
DECIDED TO GO TO BLACK HOUSE SO SHE
COULD BE HELD AND LAY IN HIS ARMS
BUT A ARGUMENT HAPPENED AND
KENEKA ENDED UP LEAVING BLACK
AGAIN SHE WAS ALREADY AT HER
LOWEST AND BLACK WASN'T HELPING
HER AT ALL WITH ALL THE EXTRA STUFF
KENEKA KNEW HE WAS BIPOLAR AND
HAD A AVM ON HIS BRAIN THAT MESSED

WITH HIS ANGER SHE STILL HAD A HARD TIME DEALING WITH HIM AT TIMES BUT THE LOVE SHE HAD FOR HIM DIDN'T CHANGE SHE JUST FOUND HER SELF NEEDING A BREAK AFTER TAKING SO MUCH AND ALL KENEKA KNEW WAS RUNNING CAUSE THAT WHAT SHE DID FOR SO MANY YEARS WITH BJ KENEKA TRIED NOT TO LEAVE BUT SOMETIMES SHE FAILS SHE WANTED TO LEARN SOME NEW COPING SKILLS TO DEAL WITH BLACK CAUSE SHE REALLY DID LOVE HIM AND IT WASN'T JUST LOVE SHE WAS IN LOVE WITH HIM AND HAD BEEN SINCE BACK IN 1997 SO KENEKA AND BLACK WHERE SEPARATED FOR A WHILE

KENEKA JUST STAYED SINGLE AND
WORKED ON HER AND IN PROVING HER
DEPRESSION IT WAS NOW THE MONTH OF
MARCH KENEKA WAS STILL DOWN AND
DEPRESSED THEN KENEKA GETS A GLIDE
VIDEO CHAT MESSAGE FROM HER GOD
DAD HE ASKED HER HOW SHE WAS DOING
THEN KENEKA TOLD HIM EVERYTHING
AND HOW HER DEPRESSION WAS AT ITS
WORSE AND THAT SHE WAS ISOLATING
HER GOD DAD TOLD HER YOU NEED TO
BE AROUND PEOPLE THAT LOVE YOU
YOU SHOULD NOT ISOLATE WHEN YOUR
DEPRESSED THEN HER GOD DAD TOLD
HER HE WANTED HER TO COME IN TO
THE MONDAY MORNING MEETING AND

HE TOLD HER HE WANTED HER TO WORK IN HIS OFFICE WITH HIM SO HE COULD SEE HER MORE AND BE AROUND HER MORE SO KENEKA SAID OK BECAUSE AFTER THEY STOPPED HIM FROM DOING THE PARENTING CLASSES KENEKA WENT FROM SEEING HIM TO ONCE A WEEK TO NOT AT ALL JUST THREW VIDEO MESSAGES  ONLY AFTER HE LEFT URBAN VENTURES SO A FEW DAYS PAST AND KENEKA SHOWED UP FOR THE MORNING MEETING AT HER GOD DADS OFFICE AFTER THE MEETING WAS OVER HER GOD DAD GAVE HER A BIG HUG AND ALL THE STAFF AT MAD DADS PRAYED FOR HER THAT WAS WHAT SEE NEEDED

KENEKA HAS A LOT OF POSITIVE PEOPLE AROUND HER SHE HAD THE URBAN VENTURES STAFF CRETIN ONES AS WELL AS HER CHURCH FAMILY AND KENEKA WAS NOW SURROUNDED WITH HER GOD DADS STAFF AND GETTING TO KNOW THEM AS WELL SO AFTER THE MORNING MEETING KENEKA DID SOME WORK IN THE OFFICE FOR HER GOD DAD AND FROM THAT DAYON KENEKA SHOWED UP EVERY MONDAY MORNING TO SIT THERE THE STAFF MEETING AND DID WORK AFTER THE MEETING AT THE END OF MARCH KENEKA AND HER FAVORITE COUSIN GOT READY TO POP UP ON HER BROTHER THAT WAS DOWN IN IOWA

KENEKA REALLY NEEDED TO BE AROUND HER BROTHER SHE MISSED HIM SO MUCH AND HADN'T SEEN HIM IN 2 YEARS SO AFTER KENEKA WENT TO GET THE RENTAL SHE WENT BACK HOME TO LOAD UP THE TRUCK WITH HER AND THE KIDS STUFF THEN SHE WENT TO GRAB THE KIDS FROM SCHOOL THEN SHE WENT TO GRAB HER COUSIN AND THEY HIT THE HIGH WAY KENEKA DROVE FIRST SOON AS KENEKA HIT IOWA IT WAS LIKE THE WEIGHT OF THE WORLD LIFTED OFF HER SHOULDERS SHE WASN'T AS DEPRESSED AND SHE WAS ENJOYING THE SCENERY OF BEING ON THE ROAD IT GOT BORING AFTER A WHILE BUT HER COUSIN KEPT

HER LAUGHING WHILE THEY WHERE ON THERE WAY DOWN TO IOWA SEVERAL PEOPLE KEPT LOOKING AT US WHILE THEY WHERE DRIVING MY COUSIN WAS LIKE WHAT BLACK PEOPLE CANT DRIVE 2017 TRUCKS OR SOMETHING SHE WAS MAKING FACES AT PEOPLE AND STICKING UP HER FINGER SHE HAD KENEKA LAUGHING SO HARD HE STOMACH WAS HURTING THEY HAD A 2017 FORD EXPEDITION TRUCK THAT WAS WHITE SO THEY HAD A LOT OF PEOPLE DRIVING BY THEM LOOKING TO SEE WHO WAS DRIVING THEN THEY LOOKED AT AS LIKE THEY WAS SHOCKED KENEKA GOT A KICK OUT OF IT AND SO DID HER

COUSIN ABOUT HALF WAY TO IOWA KENEKA GOT TIRED OF DRIVING AND HER LEG WAS KILLING HER SHE GOT IN A CAR ACCIDENT AT THE AGE OF 17 SO HER LEG WASNT THE SAME ANYMORE SHE COULD ONLY DRIVE FOR SO LONG BEFORE HE LEG STARED HURTING AND GETTING NUMB SO HER COUSIN TOOK OVER THE CLOSER THEY GOT THE MORE EXCITED KENEKA GOT SHE WAS TO HAPPY THAT SHE WAS ABOUT TO SEE HER BROTHER ABOUT A HOUR LATER THEY ARRIVE AT HER BROTHERS HOUSE HER COUSIN STARTS BLOWING THE HONKING LIKE CRAZY WHEN THEY PULL UP TO THE HOUSE KENEKA LOOKS AT

HER COUSIN AND STARTS LAUGHING HER COUSIN PUTS THE TRUCK IN PARK AND THEY ALL JUMP OUT AND RUN INTO THE APARTMENT BUILDING SOON AS KENEKA GOES IN HIS APARTMENT HER BROTHER IS STANDING RIGHT AT THE DOOR AND SAYS HEY SIS AND GIVES HER A BIG BEAR HUG AND TELLS HER HES HAPPY SHE IS THERE WHILE HE IS STILL HUGGING HER KENEKA SAID ME TO SHE MISSED HIS BIG BEAR HUGS AND SHE NEEDED IT THEN WHEN HE LET HER GO SHE SAID HI TO HIS GIRL AND SHE GOT TO MEET HER NEPHEWS FOR THE FIRST TIME KENEKA WAS REALLY HAPPY THAT SHE FINALLY GOT TO SEE THEM KENEKA ALSO GOT TO

SEE HER 14 YEAR OLD NIECE THAT SHE NEVER MET FOR THE FIRST TIME AND ONE OF HER OTHER NIECES SHE ONLY SEEN ONE TIME THAT WAS NOW GROWN KENEKAS DEPRESSION HAD DISAPPEARED SOON AS SHE GOT OUT OF MINNESOTA AND AROUND HER BROTHER FOR SOME REASON BUT THAT WAS A GOOD THING KENEKA HAD A GOOD TIME WHEN SHE WAS THERE AND HER COUSIN WAS THE LIFE OF THE PARTY SHE KEPT HER LAUGHING THAT'S WHAT SHE LOVES ABOUT HER COUSIN SHE IF FUN TO BE AROUND WHILE KENEKA WAS THERE SHE GOT TO SEE PICTURES OF HER DAD THAT SHE HAD NEVER SEEN SHE HAD

ONE THAT HER MOM GAVE HER BUT HER BROTHER HAD A BUNCH OF THEM KENEKA WAS HAPPY TO SEE SOME MORE PICTURES OF HER DAD KENEKA HAD A GOOD TIME FOR THE WEEK SHE WAS DOWN THERE THEY ALSO BARBECUED THE NIGHT BEFORE KENEKA AND HER COUSIN LEAVES KENEKAS 14 YEAR OLD NIECE COMES OVER AND SPENDS THE NIGHT SHE ENJOYED HAVING US THERE AND MY KIDS LOVED PLAY WITH HER AND THERE 2 OTHER COUSINS  LATER THAT NIGHT KENEKA GOT EMOTIONAL AND STARED CRYING BECAUSE SHE HAD TO LEAVE TO GO BACK TO MINNESOTA TOMORROW AFTER NOON KENEKA

DIDN'T WANT TO GO BUT SHE HAD TO GET THE RENTAL BACK ON TIME THE NEXT MORNING WHEN EVERYONE GOT UP KENEKAS 14 YEAR OLD NIECE ASKED KENEKA CAN Y'ALL PLEASE STAY ONE MORE NIGHT KENEKA FELT BAD AND REPLIED I CANT I HAVE TO GET THE RENTAL CAR BACK ON TIME HER NIECE POKED HER LIP OUT THEN KENEKA REPLIED WE WILL BE BACK I PROMISE AND WILL COME GET YOU THE DAY I GET HERE IN THE SUMMER OK HER NIECE REPLIED OK SOON AS 11PM HIT KENEKA MADE THE KIDS LUNCH BEFORE THEY HIT THE ROAD AT 12PM AND THEY ALL TOOK PICTURES TOGETHER BEFORE

THEY LEFT THEN THEY STARTED TO LOAD UP THE CAR AND HIT THE HIGHWAY KENEKA DECIDE TO TRY AND PUSH HER SELF ON THE WAY BACK AND DRIVE THE WHOLE WAY BACK KENEKA ENDED UP DOING THE WHOLE DRIVE SHE TOOK SOME PAIN KILLERS FOR HER LEG AND SHE WAS OK KENEKA ENDED UP MAKING IT ALL THE WAY BACK TO MINNESOTA SHE WAS GLAD TO SEE SHE COULD DO IT ONCE KENEKA AND HER COUSIN GOT BACK KENEKA DROPPED HER COUSIN OFF AT HER HOUSE AND HEADED HOME ONCE KENEKA ARRIVED AT HER HOUSE SHE UN LOADED THE TRUCK AND WENT IN THE HOUSE AND

GOT SETTLED IN AND GOT THE KIDS IN BED THEN KENEKA LAY ED DOWN AS WELL SHE WAS MISSING HER BROTHER ALREADY AND SHE JUST LEFT HIM SHE PULLED OUT HER PHONE AND KEPT LOOKING AT THE PICTURES THEY TOOK TOGETHER THEN KENEKA BEGIN TO THINK ABOUT WHEN SHE WANTED TO GO BACK DOWN THERE SO KENEKA WENT ON THE CAR RENTAL APP SHE HAD ON HER PHONE AND LOOKED AT THE PRICE FOR WHAT IT WOULD COST FOR A RENTAL IN JUNE THE WEEK OF HER BROTHERS BIRTHDAY IT WAS 205.00 DOLLAR'S SO KENEKA BOOKED IT THE NEXT MORNING KENEKA GOT UP AND

GOT READY FOR CHURCH AND WENT AND GOT HER MOM AND HEADED TO CHURCH AFTER SERVICE WAS OVER KENEKA DROPPED HER NON OFF AND HEADED BACK HOME SHE HAD TO RETURN THE RENTAL BY 5PM SHE DIDN'T WANT TO SHE HAD FEEL IN LOVE WITH THE 2017 TRUCK WHEN KENEKA RETURNED IT SHE GOT A RIDE BACK HOME AND GOT THE KIDS CLOTHES WASHED FOR SCHOOL IN THE MORNING THE NEXT MORNING KENEKA GOT THE KIDS OFF TO SCHOOL AND HEADED IN TO THE OFFICE AT MAD DADS FOR THE MORNING MEETING AND DID HER HOURS AFTER THE MORNING MEETING ABOUT 3

WEEKS LATER IT WAS NOW APRIL 11TH
2017 KENEKA BEGIN TO THINK ABOUT
BLACK A WHOLE LOT HIS BIRTHDAY WAS
THE NEXT DAY SO KENEKA WAS REALLY
STARING TO GET IN HER FEELINGS THE
NEXT MORNING KENEKA TEXT HIM AND
SAID HAPPY BIRTHDAY ! BLACK REPLIED
THANKS AFTER KENEKA PUT THE KIDS
ON THE BUS SHE WENT TO SUPER
AMERICA TO GET HER 32 OUNCE
MOUNTIN  DEW LIKE SHE DOES EVERY
MORNING THEN KENEKA HEADED TO 7
MILE TO FIND HIM A COUPLE OUTFITS
THEN KENEKA WENT TO TARGET AND
GOT HIM A CHOCOLATE CAKE AND CARD
FOR HIS BIRTHDAY THEN KENEKA

TEXTED BLACK AND TOLD HIM TO STOP BY BLACK REPLIED WHY THEN KENEKA REPLIED JUST DO IT PLEASE THEN BLACK REPLIED OK THEN KENEKA LEFT THE STORE AND HEADED BACK TO HER HOUSE TO GET THE KIDS OFF THE BUS AND THEN SHE WENT HOME TO MAKE THEM DINNER ABOUT A HOUR LATER BLACK SHOWED UP THE KIDS SEEN HIM COMING AND RAN OUT THE HOUSE TO OPEN THE DOOR FOR HIM WHEN BLACK CAME IN THE HOUSE KENEKA HANDED HIM HIS BAG FULL OF GIFTS AND SAID HAPPY BIRTHDAY !!! BLACK LOOKS AT HER WITH A SHOCKED LOOK ON HIS FACE AND TAKES THE BAG AND SAYS

THANKS BUT WHY YOU DOING THIS ???
KENEKA THEN REPLIES BECAUSE ITS
YOUR BIRTHDAY THEN BLACK PUTS THE
BAG DOWN ON THE COUCH AND SAYS TO
KENEKA CAN I TALK TO YOU FOR A
MINUTE KENEKA SAYS OK THEN BLACK
STARTS WALKING BACK TO HER
BEDROOM KENEKA FOLLOWS HIM THEN
CLOSES THE BEDROOM DOOR BEHIND
HER THEN BLACK ASKED KENEKA YOU
STILL LOVE ME DON'T YOU KENEKA JUST
LOOKS AT HIM FOR A SECOND AND SHE
KNEW SHE COULDN'T SAY NO CAUSE SHE
WOULD BE LIEING KENEKA TOOK A DEEP
BREATH AND SAID YES ... BLACK SMILES
AND SAYS OK WE CAN GET BACK

TOGETHER THEN KENEKA AND BLACK GO BACK IN THE LIVING ROOM WITH THE KIDS BLACK SITS DOWN AND LOOKS AT THE STUFF KENEKA GOT HIM AND OPENS HIS CARD THEN TELLS KENEKA THANK YOU KENEKA REPLIES YOUR WELCOME THEN THE KIDS BEGIN TALKING TO HIM ABOUT EVERYTHING UNDER THE SUN THEY WHERE HAPPY TO SEE HIM AGAIN BLACK STAYED FOR ABOUT A HOUR THEN HE LEFT ABOUT A WEEK LATER KENEKA SAYS TO BLACK I THINK WE SHOULD DO COUPLES COUNSELING BLACK AGREED TO DO IT SO KENEKA SET IT UP AND THEY BEGIN TO DO THERE COUNSELING IT WAS

GOING GOOD AND THEY KEPT GOING
AND KENEKA KEPT GOING TO CHURCH
AND BEING AROUND HER GOD DAD AND
WORKING IN HIS OFFICE AND GOING TO
CHURCH LIKE SHE WAS DOING AND
KENEKA ALSO BEGIN TO TRY HARDER ON
WORKING THREW PROBLEMS WITH
BLACK BECAUSE SHE LOVES HIM AND
SHE REALLY WANTS IT TO WORK
AROUND THE END OF MAY KENEKAS GOD
DAD TOLD HER HE WAS WRITING A BOOK
AND THAT INSPIRED KENEKA TO TELL
HER STORY AS WELL HER GOD DAD WAS
RUBBING OFF ON HER IN ALOT OF WAYS
SO KENEKA STARTED WRITING A BOOK
ABOUT HER LIFE ON HER LAB TOP AND

SHE WAS EXCITED ABOUT IT DESPITE WHAT KENEKA HAD BEEN THREW SHE WOULD ALLWAYS KEEP HER HEAD UP AND KEEP FIGHTING SHE KEPT POSITIVE PEOPLE AROUND HER TO KEEP HER ENCOURAGED AND SHE STAYED IN CHURCH SO HAVING THEM POSITIVE PEOPLE IN HER CIRCLE AND HER CHURCH HELPED HER STAY GROUNDED EVEN WHEN SHE WAS AT HER WORST SHE CAME OUT OF IT AND BEING FIGHTING AGAIN AND STRIVING FOR THE GOOD THINGS IN LIFE SHE ALSO HAD TO FORGIVE THE PEOPLE WHO HURT HER NOT FOR THEM BUT FOR HER AND HER HEALING PROCESS SOON AS KENEKA

BEGIN TO FORGIVE THE PEOPLE SHE
DIDN'T WANT TO FORGIVE IT WAS LIKE
THE WEIGHT LIFTED OFF HER
SHOULDERS IT WAS A VERY LONG
PROCESS FOR KENEKA TO ACTUALLY
FORGIVE HER MOM AND THE MAN THAT
TOUCHED HER BUT WITH THE WORD OF
GOD AND GETTING PROFESSIONAL HELP
KENEKA WAS NOW AT A PLACE IN HER
LIFE WHERE SHE COULD TALK ABOUT
WHAT HAPPENED TO HER AS A CHILD
WITH OUT CRYING SHE STILL HAS
DREAMS ABOUT IT BUT SHE STILL HAS
DONE A WHOLE LOT OF HEALING AS
WELL AND SHE NOW HAS A BETTER
RELATIONSHIP WITH HER MOM SHE

DIDN'T LIKE HER MOM FOR MANY YEARS BUT WHEN SHE BEGIN TO LEAN TO FORGIVE THAT'S WHEN THINGS SLOWLY GOT BETTER BETWEEN HER AND HER MOM HER MOM STARTED ATTENDING CHURCH WITH KENEKA AND NOW THERE RELATIONSHIP IS BETTER THAN IT HAD BEEN FOR MANY YEARS AND KENEKA AND BLACK ARE CONTINUING TO WORK ON THERE RELATIONSHIP ITS WHAT THEY BOTH WANT CAUSE THEY ARE VERY IN LOVE WITH EACH OTHER AND THEY BOTH DON'T WANT TO START OVER WITH NO ONE ELSE SO THEY WILL KEEP ON WORKING ON GETTING IT RIGHT AND KENEKA WILL CONTINUE WORK WITH

HER GOD DAD IN HIS OFFICE AND
WORKING ON GROWING HER BUSINESS
AND SHE WILL ALSO KEEP WORKING ON
HER GROWTH.


# " *THE END* "

66292173R00165

Made in the USA
Lexington, KY
09 August 2017